Smart Business, Smart Credit

"A Practical Guide to Enhancing Financial Literacy and Building Business Credit"

Shameka Landers

COPYRIGHT STATEMENT

All rights reserved by the author.

No portion of this book may be reproduced, distributed, or transmitted in any form, including but not limited to recording, photocopying, mechanical, or electronic methods, without prior written consent from the author. Any unauthorized use, duplication, or distribution of this work is strictly prohibited and may lead to legal consequences.

The author and publisher make no guarantees regarding the accuracy of the information presented, as outcomes may vary based on individual circumstances and context.

Smart Business, Smart Credit

Shameka Landers

PREFACE

Success in business is rarely accidental. It is the result of deliberate actions, strategic planning, and a relentless commitment to growth. Whether you are a first-time entrepreneur or a seasoned business owner looking to expand, the notion of business credit is both necessary and empowering. However, for many, it remains an enigma—a subject that is frequently disregarded or misunderstood. That is where this book comes in.

Smart Business, Smart Credit is more than a guide; it's a toolkit for transformation. It bridges the gap between foundational financial knowledge and actionable strategies that can propel your business to new heights. Building business credit is not just about securing loans or improving cash flow; it's about establishing credibility, protecting your personal assets, and creating opportunities for sustainable growth.

Over the years, I've seen countless entrepreneurs struggle with financing, often relying on personal credit to fund their dreams. This approach, while it's common, is fraught with risks. Mixing personal and business finances can limit your growth potential and expose your personal assets to unnecessary liabilities. The solution lies in creating a robust business credit profile—a cornerstone of financial independence and strategic growth.

This book is divided into three comprehensive parts, each designed to address key aspects of business credit and smart practices. In the first section, we'll understand the foundations of business credit—what it is, why it matters, and how to establish it. You'll learn the importance of setting up your business correctly, from registering with the right agencies to building your initial trade lines.

Shameka Landers

The second section will be about leveraging business credit for growth. Here, we'll explore how to use credit strategically to scale your operations, invest in new opportunities, and secure long-term financial stability. Real-life case studies will illustrate how entrepreneurs have turned credit into a powerful tool for expansion.

Finally, the third section introduces advanced strategies and practices for managing and protecting your credit profile. From monitoring your scores to mitigating risks, these chapters will provide you with the insights needed to navigate the complexities of business credit in an ever-evolving landscape. We'll also discuss the future of business credit, including trends like fintech innovations and sustainable lending practices.

Throughout this journey, my goal is to ensure that every chapter resonates with actionable insights. This is not a theoretical discourse—it's a practical guide meant to empower you to take control of your financial future. By the end of this book, you'll have the tools, knowledge, and confidence to build a thriving business backed by a strong credit foundation.

Entrepreneurship is a journey of resilience, creativity, and constant learning. As you turn these pages, I encourage you to approach each chapter with curiosity and determination. Your success story is waiting to be written, and it begins with the decisions you make today. Let *Smart Business, Smart Credit* be your trusted companion as you build the business and life you've always envisioned.

Here's to your success and the limitless potential of smart business practices. Let's get started.

Shameka Landers

TABLE OF CONTENTS

COPYRIGHT STATEMENT II
PREFACE IV
TABLE OF CONTENTS VI
THE BASICS OF BUSINESS CREDIT 1
    What Is Business Credit? 2
    Why Business Credit Matters 4
    Key Components of Business Credit 5
    Common Misconceptions About Business Credit 7
ESTABLISHING YOUR BUSINESS CREDIT PROFILE
.... 10
    Step 1: Formalize Your Business 10
    Step 2: Set Up Professional Operations 11
    Step 3: Register with Business Credit Bureaus 12
    Step 4: Establish Trade Lines with Vendors 12
    Step 5: Use Business Credit Cards Responsibly 13
    Step 6: Monitor and Protect Your Credit Profile 13
UNDERSTANDING BUSINESS CREDIT SCORES 15
    What Are Business Credit Scores? 15
    Key Components of Business Credit Scores 16
    How to monitor your business credit score 18
    Steps to Improve Your Business Credit Scores 20
    Common Mistakes to Avoid 22
TRADE LINES AND VENDOR ACCOUNTS 25
    What Are Trade Lines? 25

Setting Up Vendor Accounts..27
Types of Trade Lines to Establish 30
Best Practices for Managing Trade Lines 33
The Long-Term Benefits of Trade Lines..............................35

LEVERAGING BUSINESS CREDIT FOR GROWTH....37
Understanding the Power of Business Credit.....................38
Types of Financing to Leverage 39
Strategies for Leveraging Credit Wisely 43
Real-Life Case Studies...44
The Risks of Mismanaging Business Credit 45

SCALING YOUR BUSINESS WITH BUSINESS CREDIT 47
Strategic Use of Business Credit..48
Tips for Sustainable Growth Using Business Credit..........50
Balancing Debt and Risk 52

MANAGING DEBT AND AVOIDING COMMON PITFALLS...55
Common Credit Management Mistakes 56
Proactive Credit Management Strategies 60
Key Takeaways..64

SMART FINANCIAL MANAGEMENT 66
Key Takeaways..72

THE FUTURE OF BUSINESS CREDIT................................73
How Business Credit is Evolving..74
Emerging Financial Technologies Shaping Business Credit 75

Shameka Landers

How Your Business Can Prepare for the Future of Credit 79

LEVERAGING CREDIT FOR COMPETITIVE ADVANTAGE 84

The Role of Credit in Gaining Market Advantage 85

Using Credit to Outpace Competitors 86

Leveraging Credit for International Expansion 88

Strategies for Building Global Credit 89

Enhancing Customer Acquisition Through Financial Strength 91

Strategic Considerations and Risk Management 93

Crafting Your Personal Credit Strategy for Competitive Growth 96

Conclusion 99

RISK MANAGEMENT IN CREDIT USE 101

Understanding the Nature of Credit Risk 101

Strategies for Mitigating Credit Risk 102

Building a Culture of Proactive Risk Management 107

USING BUSINESS CREDIT TO IMPROVE OPERATIONS 109

The Intersection of Credit and Operational Efficiency .. 109

Investing in Technology and Automation 111

Strategies to Optimize Processes with Credit 112

Enhancing Supply Chain Efficiency 113

Conclusion 114

HOW SUCCESSFUL ENTREPRENEURS USE BUSINESS CREDIT 115

Leveraging Business Credit for Expansion and Scalability 115

Strengthening Supplier Relationships Through Smart Credit Management 117

Using Credit to Fund Innovation and Competitive Differentiation 118

Conclusion 120

SMART LEADERSHIP AND TEAM MANAGEMENT 121

Traits of Financially Savvy Leaders 121

Building Financial Literacy Within Leadership Teams 124

TRANSITIONING FROM CREDIT RELIANCE TO FINANCIAL INDEPENDENCE 127

The Signs Your Business is Ready to Rely Less on Credit 127

Strategies for Reducing Credit Dependence 129

Leveraging Credit for Growth Without Dependency 131

The Long-Term Benefits of Financial Independence 132

THE LEGACY OF SMART CREDIT USE 134

The Role of Credit in Building a Lasting Business Legacy 134

Strategies for Sustainable Credit Use 135

The Impact of Responsible Credit Use on Business Reputation 138

CONCLUSION 139

Reflecting on the Bigger Picture 141

Key Reflections and Takeaways 144

A Call to Action 144

Smart Business, Smart Credit

Shameka Landers

1

THE BASICS OF BUSINESS CREDIT

Success in business is 90% preparation and 10% credit.

Business credit is the cornerstone of any thriving enterprise. It serves not just as a financial tool but as the bedrock for scalability, innovation, and long-term growth. When wielded effectively, business credit empowers entrepreneurs to unlock opportunities that might otherwise remain inaccessible.

This section of the book explores the essence of business credit, outlining its critical role in enabling success. From securing capital for expansion to establishing a professional image that fosters trust, the significance of business credit cannot be overstated. Understanding its nuances is the first decisive step in transforming your entrepreneurial vision into a reality. Together, we will delve into why business credit matters, its key components, and how to build a profile that gives your business a competitive edge.

Shameka Landers

WHAT IS BUSINESS CREDIT?

Business credit refers to a company's ability to secure financing based on its financial reputation. Imagine your business as a growing plant in an entrepreneurial garden. The quality of its soil, the water it receives, and the care it gets all influence its ability to thrive. Business credit is akin to the rich, fertile soil that sustains and nurtures your enterprise.

Unlike personal credit—which assesses an individual's reliability to repay loans—business credit is tied to your Employer Identification Number (EIN). This distinction is crucial for building financial independence and ensuring the longevity of your operations. It is more than a protective layer for your personal assets; it is a badge of credibility for your company. With strong business credit, your enterprise is more likely to attract favorable terms from lenders and vendors who see a stable, trustworthy partner.

Consider this: When a supplier evaluates your business, they're not merely selling goods; they're investing in your reliability to pay them back. Business credit serves as their assurance. It's a testament to how your company manages its financial obligations, maintains transparency, and meets commitments.

Beyond the numbers, business credit reflects the discipline of your operations. It's shaped by key factors like timely payments, responsible credit utilization, and how your company handles public financial records. A vendor extending net 30 terms or a lender approving a new line of credit will look at this score as an indicator of future transactions.

Visualize the power of a robust credit profile this way – it's like walking into a room with a glowing reputation that precedes you. Vendors and suppliers are eager to work with you and are confident in your ability to deliver on agreements. It's the

Shameka Landers

difference between negotiating from a position of strength versus struggling to prove your worth.

In essence, business credit is not just about borrowing money. It's about building trust—the currency of commerce—and positioning your business as a reliable and professional entity. When managed effectively, it becomes a tool for growth, paving the way for opportunities that extend far beyond financial transactions. Unlike personal credit, which is tied to your Social Security Number (SSN), business credit is connected to your Employer Identification Number (EIN). This critical distinction offers numerous advantages, with the most notable being the separation of personal and business financial activities. By segregating these financial domains, entrepreneurs safeguard their personal assets, mitigate liability risks, and reinforce the financial independence of their businesses.

Business credit evaluates the financial health and responsibility of a company. Unlike personal credit, which focuses solely on an individual's creditworthiness, business credit provides a lens into the operational and fiscal discipline of an enterprise. Factors such as timely payments, credit utilization, and financial transparency play pivotal roles in shaping a company's credit profile.

Lenders, suppliers, and vendors heavily rely on business credit scores to assess risk before extending credit, entering into agreements, or forming partnerships. A strong credit profile signals financial stability, reliability, and a lower probability of default, making it easier to secure favorable terms and unlock growth opportunities.

Shameka Landers

WHY BUSINESS CREDIT MATTERS

You need to understand the significance of business credit before you can unlock its full potential. The following are compelling reasons why building and maintaining business credit should be your priority as an entrepreneur:

- **Access to Capital:** Imagine having the financial flexibility to seize opportunities the moment they arise. Business credit makes this possible by enabling you to secure loans, credit lines, and better payment terms. Whether it's expanding your product line, purchasing inventory, or upgrading your technology, access to capital fuels growth and innovation. Think of it as the engine that powers your business forward, allowing you to navigate challenges and scale effectively.

- **Separation of Finances:** Mixing personal and business finances is a recipe for confusion and potential disaster in your business. Having business credit allows you to draw a clear line between your personal and professional financial activities. This separation is not only a safeguard for your personal assets but also simplifies tax preparation and financial reporting. By doing so, you set your business up for long-term sustainability while minimizing personal liability.

- **Professional Image:** First impressions matter, especially in business. A good credit profile sends a strong message to vendors, suppliers, and lenders that your business is credible, financially responsible, and worth trusting. This professional image can open doors to better deals, partnerships, and terms, positioning your company as a reliable player in the market.

- **Lower Interest Rates:** The strength of your business credit score directly impacts the cost of borrowing. A higher score often translates to lower interest rates, reduced borrowing costs, and better repayment terms. This means you can reinvest savings back into your business, boosting profitability and fostering growth. Imagine the competitive advantage of accessing capital at favorable rates while your competitors struggle with higher costs.

- **Business Growth:** Growth is the ultimate goal for any business, and good credit provides the foundation for scaling. Whether it's hiring staff, opening new locations, or covering operational costs, strong business credit offers the financial flexibility to turn ambitious plans into reality. It's the key to unlocking potential and staying ahead in a competitive market.

These reasons show the transformative power of business credit. It's more than a financial tool; it's a strategic asset that enables you to build, sustain, and grow your enterprise. By understanding and prioritizing business credit, you can pave the way for enduring success.

KEY COMPONENTS OF BUSINESS CREDIT

Building business credit requires a clear understanding of its fundamental components. Each element of it acts as a building block for creating a reliable credit profile that sets your business apart from competitors.

1. **Credit Scores:** Think of credit scores as the report cards of your business's financial health. These scores provide a snapshot of how well your business manages its credit responsibilities:

- *Dun & Bradstreet PAYDEX:* Ranging from 0 to 100, a score above 80 signifies excellent payment performance. This metric heavily influences vendor and supplier trust.

  - *Experian Intelliscore:* Factors such as payment history, industry risk, and public records are used to gauge the financial stability of your enterprise.

  - *Equifax Business Credit Risk Score:* This score predicts the likelihood of late payments, helping lenders assess risk before extending credit.

2. **Payment History:** Payment history is the core of your credit profile. Timely payments to creditors, suppliers, and lenders establish trust and reliability. Late payments, on the other hand, can tarnish your reputation and negatively impact your scores.

3. **Credit Utilization:** A low credit utilization ratio—the percentage of available credit your business is using—signals financial stability and prudent credit management. Strive to keep this ratio below 30% to demonstrate responsible credit use.

4. **Public Records:** Public records such as bankruptcies, liens, and judgments are red flags that can severely damage your credit profile. Maintaining clean public records is essential for safeguarding your business's financial reputation.

If you can actively manage these components, your business will build a strong credit foundation that not only supports growth but also enhances credibility in the eyes of lenders,

Shameka Landers

suppliers, and partners. Your understanding of these elements is your first step towards crafting a thriving financial future for your business.

COMMON MISCONCEPTIONS ABOUT BUSINESS CREDIT

Despite its importance, many entrepreneurs have harbored misconceptions about business credit. Let me address these myths and talk about the realities:

1. **Myth:** Business credit is the same as personal credit.

    - *Reality:* While business and personal credit share some similarities, they are fundamentally different. Personal credit evaluates your individual financial habits and is tied to your Social Security Number (SSN). Business credit, on the other hand, assesses the financial health of your company and is tied to your Employer Identification Number (EIN). This distinction ensures that your personal finances remain separate from your business operations, offering both protection and clarity.

2. **Myth:** Only large corporations need business credit.

    - *Reality:* Business credit is just as important for small businesses as it is for large corporations. Small enterprises often face tighter cash flow constraints, and having access to credit can make a significant difference. Whether it's negotiating favorable terms with suppliers or securing funds to manage unexpected expenses, a strong business credit profile can provide the flexibility needed to thrive in competitive markets.

3. **Myth:** Building business credit takes years.

    - *Reality:* Establishing business credit doesn't have to be a long, drawn-out process. With a focused strategy and consistent effort, you can start building a solid credit profile within months. By setting up trade lines with vendors who report to credit bureaus, paying bills on time, and maintaining financial discipline, even new businesses can see progress quickly.

4. **Myth:** Business credit is only needed for loans.

    - *Reality:* While credit is essential for securing loans, its utility extends far beyond borrowing. Business credit affects your relationships with suppliers, the terms you receive on payments, and even your ability to negotiate leases for office space or equipment. It's a comprehensive measure of your company's reliability and financial health, influencing how others choose to work with you.

5. **Myth:** Personal credit can replace business credit.

    - *Reality:* Relying solely on personal credit for business needs exposes you to unnecessary risks. High utilization of personal credit cards or loans taken for business purposes can negatively impact your personal credit score, limiting your financial options in both realms. Building business credit allows you to keep personal and professional finances distinct, ensuring the stability of both.

By debunking these myths, entrepreneurs can approach business credit with a clearer understanding of its importance and potential. Developing a strong credit profile is not just for established corporations—it's an essential step for businesses of all sizes seeking to grow and succeed.

Understanding and leveraging business credit is a game-changer for entrepreneurs. It not only unlocks opportunities but also fortifies the financial stability of your enterprise. By laying a strong credit foundation and actively managing it, you position your business for sustained success.

This chapter has set the stage for your journey into the reality of business credit. In the next chapter, I will expose you to the practical steps to establish your business credit profile, ensuring that you have the tools and knowledge to build a thriving financial future.

2

ESTABLISHING YOUR BUSINESS CREDIT PROFILE

A strong foundation builds a strong business

Building a business credit profile is like laying the first brick of a sturdy building. It requires precision, foresight, and a commitment to doing things the right way. Establishing business credit not only safeguards your personal finances but also opens doors to opportunities that can move your business toward growth and stability. Let me walk you through the essential steps and strategies to create a robust business credit profile.

STEP 1: FORMALIZE YOUR BUSINESS

Before you can build credit, your business needs to be properly structured and recognized as a separate entity. Here's how:

- **Choose the Right Business Structure:** Decide whether your business will operate as an LLC, corporation, or partnership. Each structure has its advantages, but all provide the legal separation necessary to build business credit.

- **Obtain an EIN:** Think of your Employer Identification Number (EIN) as your business's Social Security Number. It's required for opening business accounts and filing taxes, and it's the foundation for building your credit profile.

- **Register Your Business:** Ensure your business is properly registered with your state or local government. This establishes its legitimacy and sets the stage for working with vendors and credit bureaus.

- **Open a Business Bank Account:** A dedicated bank account separates your business transactions from personal ones. This step not only simplifies accounting but also signals to lenders and suppliers that your business is serious and professional.

STEP 2: SET UP PROFESSIONAL OPERATIONS

The way you present your business matters. Lenders and suppliers want to work with companies that appear credible and trustworthy. Here are key steps to enhance your professional image:

- **Have an Address and Phone Number:** Use a business address and dedicated phone line rather than personal contact information. Virtual offices or coworking spaces can serve as professional addresses for startups.

- **Create a Consistent Online Presence:** Ensure that your business name, address, and phone number are consistent across all platforms, including your website, social media, and official documents. Inconsistencies can raise red flags for credit bureaus.

- **Get Listed in Business Directories:** Register your company with directories like Google My Business, Yelp, and industry-specific platforms. Being discoverable online adds credibility.

STEP 3: REGISTER WITH BUSINESS CREDIT BUREAUS

To build your credit profile, your business must be visible to credit bureaus. Start by registering with the following:

- **Dun & Bradstreet (D&B):** Obtain a D-U-N-S number, a unique identifier used by D&B to track your business's credit activity. Many vendors and lenders report payment data directly to D&B, making it an essential component of your profile.

- **Experian and Equifax:** Verify your business information with these bureaus to ensure your profile is accurate. Regularly monitor these reports to catch errors or discrepancies early.

STEP 4: ESTABLISH TRADE LINES WITH VENDORS

Trade lines are agreements with suppliers that allow you to purchase goods or services on credit, with payment due at a later date. These relationships are pivotal for building your credit history. Here's how to get started:

- **Work with Vendors That Report to Credit Bureaus:** Not all vendors report payment data, so choose those who do. Examples include Uline, Quill, and Grainger.

- **Maintain a Positive Payment History:** Pay invoices on time or, better yet, early. Prompt payments demonstrate financial responsibility and improve your credit score.

- **Start Small and Scale Up:** Begin with modest credit amounts and gradually increase your trade lines as your business grows.

STEP 5: USE BUSINESS CREDIT CARDS RESPONSIBLY

Business credit cards are an excellent tool for building credit, but they must be used wisely:

- **Choose Beginner-Friendly Cards:** Opt for cards designed for new businesses, such as the Capital One Spark Classic or American Express Blue Business Cash Card.

- **Keep Balances Low:** Aim to use less than 30% of your available credit limit. High utilization can harm your credit score.

- **Pay Balances in Full:** Whenever possible, pay your balance in full each month to avoid interest charges and demonstrate financial discipline.

STEP 6: MONITOR AND PROTECT YOUR CREDIT PROFILE

Building credit is an ongoing process that requires vigilance. Here's how to stay on top of your credit profile:

- **Regularly Check Your Reports:** Use tools like Nav or CreditSignal to monitor your business credit scores. Identify and dispute inaccuracies promptly.

- **Secure Your Business Against Fraud:** Implement fraud alerts and monitor your accounts for unauthorized activity. Protecting your credit profile is as important as building it.

Establishing a business credit profile is a journey that requires dedication, strategic planning, and a clear vision of your goals. Each step you take—from formalizing your business structure to responsibly managing credit cards—lays the foundation for a thriving enterprise. By building a strong credit profile, you're not just preparing for today's needs; you're creating a financial safety net and a springboard for future opportunities. This process is more than a task; it's a strategic investment in your business's long-term growth and resilience.

3

UNDERSTANDING BUSINESS CREDIT SCORES

What gets measured gets managed

Building a strong credit profile is just the beginning. To unlock the full potential of business credit, you must understand how credit scores work and what they mean for your company's financial health. Business credit scores are more than just numbers—they are indicators of your company's reliability, financial discipline, and risk level. This chapter will help you to understand credit scoring systems, explain their components, and provide actionable steps to improve and maintain strong scores.

WHAT ARE BUSINESS CREDIT SCORES?

Business credit scores are the barometers of your company's financial reputation. They provide a window into how well your business meets its financial obligations and offer invaluable insights to lenders, vendors, and potential partners. These scores are critical because they determine your company's creditworthiness, reliability, and ability to manage risk effectively.

Unlike personal credit scores, which range from 300 to 850, business credit scores vary depending on the bureau. Here's how the major scoring systems work:

- **Dun & Bradstreet PAYDEX:** This score ranges from 0 to 100, focusing exclusively on payment history. A score above 80 signifies excellent performance, reflecting timely payments that build trust with creditors and suppliers.

- **Experian Intelliscore Plus:** Ranging from 0 to 100, this score evaluates payment history, public records, and the inherent risks associated with your industry. It provides a holistic view of your business's financial behavior.

- **Equifax Business Credit Risk Score:** With scores spanning from 101 to 992, this system predicts the likelihood of late payments. It's a comprehensive measure of financial health and operational reliability.

Each of these scores serves as a unique lens, highlighting different aspects of your financial conduct. Think of them as mirrors that reflect your business's habits and discipline. The clearer your financial actions—like paying bills on time and keeping public records clean—the better your reflection. Strong scores act as your business's calling card, showcasing its stability and trustworthiness to the world.

KEY COMPONENTS OF BUSINESS CREDIT SCORES

Imagine a situation where you walk into a meeting with a potential supplier or lender, and they already have a snapshot of your business's reliability and financial behavior. That snapshot is your business credit score—a financial report card that shapes not only your reputation but also your future opportunities. Think of it as the equivalent of a handshake in the business world, offering an immediate impression of your company's credibility and trustworthiness.

Understanding what influences your business credit scores is essential for proactively managing them and building a foundation for success. These key components form the backbone of a solid credit profile and play a pivotal role in how your business is perceived by lenders, vendors, and potential partners. By mastering these elements, you gain the ability to open doors to better financing options, stronger supplier relationships, and long-term growth.

- **Payment History:** A good credit profile is mostly dependent on payment consistency. While delays undermine confidence, every timely payment builds it. Vendors and lenders pay close attention to how consistently you satisfy your financial responsibilities. Even a single late payment might have a cascading impact, lowering your chances of obtaining favorable terms.

- **Credit Utilization:** This ratio—the amount of credit used compared to the total credit available—is a significant indicator of financial responsibility. Keeping utilization below 30% demonstrates that your business can manage resources without over-reliance on credit. Low utilization rates suggest stability, while high rates can signal financial strain, even if payments are made on time.

- **Public Records:** Issues like bankruptcies, liens, or judgments serve as red flags to potential lenders. A clean public record is a testament to your business's integrity and stability. Conversely, negative records can create hurdles when seeking financing or negotiating with suppliers.

- **Business Age:** Longevity often equates to reliability. Older businesses with established credit histories are viewed as lower risk. However, even newer businesses can build credibility by maintaining consistent financial practices and proactively managing their credit profiles.

- **Industry Risk:** Your business's industry can influence how your credit is perceived. Some industries, such as construction or hospitality, are inherently riskier in the eyes of lenders due to market volatility. While you can't change your industry, demonstrating exceptional financial management within a high-risk category can offset some of this perceived instability.

Each of these factors interacts to create a holistic picture of your business's financial health. By addressing each component proactively, you can build a credit profile that not only supports your current operations but also sets the stage for long-term growth and resilience. Your business's industry can influence how your credit is perceived. Some industries are inherently riskier, and this may affect your scores regardless of your individual performance.

HOW TO MONITOR YOUR BUSINESS CREDIT SCORE

As a continuation of the imagination that I have asked you to have in the previous section – components of business credit scores, assume that immediately you were noticed by your potential supplier or lender you now discovered inaccuracies in your business credit report that jeopardize your plans. There is nothing as bad as that, right? Yes!

Regularly monitoring your credit scores isn't just a good habit—it's a proactive measure to safeguard your financial health and business opportunities. Staying informed about your scores ensures that you're always ready to make the most of any opportunity that comes your way.

- **Access Reports from Major Bureaus:** The first step in monitoring your credit is knowing where to look. Obtain detailed credit reports from Dun & Bradstreet, Experian, and Equifax. Each bureau offers unique insights into your business's credit profile, including payment histories, credit utilization, and public records. Reviewing all three ensures you have a comprehensive understanding of how your business is viewed by creditors.

- **Use Monitoring Tools:** Simplify the process by leveraging platforms like Nav, CreditSignal, or Experian Business Credit Advantage. These tools provide real-time alerts, updates on score changes, and summaries of your credit activity. With these services, you can quickly identify improvements or spot potential issues before they escalate.

- **Review for Accuracy:** Errors in your credit reports can have serious consequences. Mistakes like outdated information, misreported payment histories, or accounts that don't belong to your business can lower your score and hinder your growth. Make it a point to regularly scrutinize your reports for inaccuracies and dispute any errors promptly. Many credit bureaus offer online portals to simplify the dispute process, ensuring that corrections are made efficiently.

By staying vigilant, you're not just protecting your credit profile—you're positioning your business for greater financial flexibility, better terms, and stronger relationships with lenders and suppliers.

STEPS TO IMPROVE YOUR BUSINESS CREDIT SCORES

Improving your business credit scores requires a multifaceted approach. Each action you take contributes to building a stronger financial foundation and unlocking greater opportunities. Here are detailed steps to elevate your credit profile:

1. **Pay Invoices Early and Consistently:** Payment history is one of the most significant factors in your credit score. Commit to paying invoices before their due dates whenever possible. Early payments not only improve your Dun & Bradstreet PAYDEX score but also strengthen relationships with vendors who may offer better terms over time.

2. **Maintain Low Credit Utilization Rates:** Aim to keep your credit utilization below 30%. This means using only a small portion of your available credit. For instance, if you have a credit line of $50,000, try not to exceed $15,000 in usage. Low utilization demonstrates financial discipline and boosts lender confidence.

3. **Open and Maintain Multiple Trade Lines:** Cultivate relationships with a diverse group of vendors that report payment activity to credit bureaus. Positive trade lines—such as those with office supply companies, wholesalers, or logistics providers—add depth to your credit profile and showcase your ability to manage multiple accounts.

Shameka Landers

4. **Monitor and Address Public Records:** Regularly review your business credit reports to identify and resolve any negative public records. Disputes, liens, or judgments can harm your score for years if not promptly addressed. Maintaining a clean record is critical to ensuring your business's credibility.

5. **Increase Credit Diversity:** Demonstrate versatility by utilizing a mix of credit products, such as short-term loans, business credit cards, and vendor accounts. A diverse credit profile signals your ability to manage different types of financial commitments effectively.

6. **Establish Credit Limits Strategically:** When applying for credit, aim for higher limits but use them responsibly. High credit limits combined with low utilization rates can significantly boost your credit scores.

7. **Avoid Frequent Credit Applications:** Limit the number of credit applications you submit within a short period. Too many inquiries can signal financial distress and negatively impact your scores. Instead, research options thoroughly and apply selectively.

8. **Maintain Longevity with Accounts:** Keep older credit accounts open, even if they are not in regular use. Longevity contributes to your credit history and demonstrates stability. Closing older accounts can shorten your credit history and lower your scores.

9. **Communicate with Creditors:** If you encounter financial difficulties, proactively communicate with creditors to negotiate payment plans. Most creditors appreciate transparency and may offer solutions that prevent late payments from being reported.

10. **Leverage Professional Credit Monitoring Services:** Enroll in services that provide real-time updates on your credit profile. These tools can alert you to changes, help you spot errors, and track your progress toward better scores.

11. **Regularly Review and Dispute Errors:** Mistakes happen. Make it a habit to review your reports from Dun & Bradstreet, Experian, and Equifax at least quarterly. Dispute any inaccuracies promptly to ensure your scores reflect accurate and up-to-date information.

12. **Build Relationships with Reporting Vendors:** Not all vendors report to credit bureaus, so prioritize those who do. Establishing long-term, positive relationships with these vendors can have a meaningful impact on your scores.

By adopting these practices, you're not just improving your credit scores—you're building a solid financial reputation that will support your business's growth and resilience.

COMMON MISTAKES TO AVOID

Even with the best intentions, mistakes can happen. Here are pitfalls to steer clear of, and strategies to help you avoid them:

- **Ignoring Credit Reports:** Regularly review your reports to catch errors or identify trends that need attention. Missing inaccuracies or outdated information can lead to unnecessary credit score reductions. Make it a habit to check reports from Dun & Bradstreet, Experian, and Equifax at least quarterly.

- **Over-Leveraging Credit:** Excessive debt or high utilization rates suggest financial instability and hurt your scores. Aim to keep your credit utilization below 30% and avoid using credit as a long-term solution for cash flow issues.

- **Neglecting Vendor Relationships:** Not all vendors report payment data. Prioritize those who do and maintain strong, positive relationships with them. Vendors who report payments to credit bureaus can significantly impact your credit profile.

- **Inconsistent Payment Practices:** Late or irregular payments damage your reputation and lower your scores. Set up automated reminders or direct debits to ensure you never miss a payment deadline.

- **Applying for Too Much Credit at Once:** Multiple credit inquiries within a short period can signal financial distress to lenders. Research thoroughly before applying, and only seek credit when necessary.

- **Closing Old Credit Accounts:** Older accounts contribute to the longevity of your credit history, which is a key factor in scoring. Even if you no longer use certain accounts, keep them open to maintain a healthy credit history.

- **Failing to Monitor Public Records:** Legal judgments, liens, or bankruptcies can devastate your credit score. Regularly check for public record updates and resolve any issues swiftly to minimize their impact.

- **Not Diversifying Credit Types:** Relying solely on one type of credit—such as business credit cards—can limit your score potential. A mix of credit types, like vendor accounts, loans, and credit cards, demonstrates financial versatility and responsible management.

- **Ignoring Fraud Alerts or Suspicious Activity:** Failing to act on potential fraud or unauthorized activities can lead to lasting damage. Implement security measures, monitor your accounts regularly, and respond to alerts promptly.

- **Relying Solely on Personal Credit:** Using personal credit to finance your business blurs financial boundaries and exposes your personal assets to risk. Establish and grow a separate business credit profile to protect your personal finances.

By staying vigilant, regularly reviewing credit reports, maintaining low credit utilization, nurturing vendor relationships, and addressing issues like public records or fraud promptly, you not only protect your credit profile but also create a solid foundation for long-term financial health, improved financing opportunities, and business success.

Business credit scores are more than metrics; they're the lifeblood of your financial reputation. By understanding the factors that influence your scores and taking proactive steps to improve them, you position your business for greater opportunities. Strong credit scores open doors to financing, partnerships, and long-term growth. In the next chapter, we'll dive into how to leverage your credit profile to secure the funding needed to fuel your ambitions.

TRADE LINES AND VENDOR ACCOUNTS

Small steps pave the way to big successes

Building business credit is like tending to a garden. Each trade line and vendor account you establish is a seed, and your efforts to nurture these relationships are the water and sunlight that help your business grow strong and resilient. Just as a gardener carefully selects the right seeds and provides the care needed for them to flourish, a business owner must choose and manage trade lines wisely. This chapter will guide you through the significance of trade lines, the vital role they play in your credit profile, and the step-by-step actions you can take to establish and cultivate them effectively. With the right approach, these financial tools can transform your business credit into a thriving ecosystem of growth and opportunity.

WHAT ARE TRADE LINES?

Trade lines are credit accounts established with suppliers, vendors, or lenders, acting as your business's lifeline to financial flexibility. They enable you to purchase goods or services on credit, with payment deferred to a later date. Think of trade lines as your business's way of demonstrating financial responsibility and reliability to the world. These accounts not only facilitate smoother operations by easing cash flow constraints but also serve as essential building blocks for your business credit history. By providing a consistent track record of your payment behaviors, trade lines report valuable data to credit bureaus, painting a picture of your company's financial discipline and trustworthiness. This, in turn, positions your business as a reliable partner in the eyes of lenders, vendors, and other stakeholders.

Why Trade Lines Matter

- **Credit History Development:** Trade lines are often the first step in establishing your business credit profile. They serve as a proving ground, demonstrating your ability to manage credit responsibly and paving the way for stronger financial partnerships.

- **Improved Credit Scores:** Positive payment histories from trade lines significantly impact your business credit scores. Every on-time payment is a building block that strengthens your financial reputation and opens doors to better opportunities.

- **Enhanced Vendor Relationships:** Strong trade line relationships can lead to better terms, discounts, and higher credit limits as trust builds over time. Vendors are more likely to offer favorable terms to businesses with a proven track record of reliability.

- **Financial Flexibility:** Trade lines offer breathing room for managing cash flow, allowing you to invest in growth while delaying payments. This flexibility is critical for navigating unexpected expenses or seizing timely opportunities.

- **Access to Larger Networks:** Establishing trade lines with key vendors often leads to introductions to broader supplier networks. This can unlock additional resources and create new avenues for business expansion.

- **Demonstration of Professionalism:** A history of responsibly managing trade lines signals to vendors and lenders that your business operates professionally, which can enhance your reputation in competitive markets.

- **Support During Economic Downturns:** Trade lines can act as a financial cushion during challenging economic periods. Reliable vendor accounts provide a safety net, ensuring your business maintains liquidity when cash flow tightens.

- **Foundation for Long-Term Growth:** Trade lines are not just about immediate benefits. They create a foundation for sustained financial health, enabling your business to scale operations, explore new markets, and invest in innovative projects with confidence.

SETTING UP VENDOR ACCOUNTS

Vendor accounts are often the easiest and most practical way to establish trade lines for your business. Think of them as the stepping stones to building a strong financial foundation. These accounts allow your business to demonstrate reliability and financial responsibility while creating opportunities for better credit terms and increased trust with suppliers. By establishing vendor accounts strategically, you can lay the groundwork for long-term business growth. Follow these steps to set them up successfully:

Step 1: Choose the Right Vendors

Selecting the right vendors is a strategic move that can make or break your efforts to build strong trade lines. Not all suppliers report payment activity to business credit bureaus, so it's essential to focus on those that do. Vendors who report help build your credit profile faster and more effectively. Here are a few trusted options to consider:

- **Uline:** Offers shipping, industrial, and retail supplies. This vendor is a favorite for businesses starting out due to their straightforward terms and reliable reporting.

- **Quill:** Specializes in office supplies and services. Their low purchase requirements make them an ideal choice for businesses just beginning to establish credit.

- **Grainger:** A leader in industrial supplies and equipment, Grainger caters to businesses that need durable goods and operational tools.

When choosing vendors, look beyond their products. Research their reporting habits to credit bureaus like Dun & Bradstreet, Experian, and Equifax. Prioritize those who consistently report payment histories, as this data is key to building your business credit profile efficiently. Start by identifying vendors that report to business credit bureaus. Not all suppliers report payment activity, so it's essential to prioritize those who do. Examples include:

- **Uline:** Offers shipping, industrial, and retail supplies.

- **Quill:** Provides office supplies and services.

- **Grainger:** Specializes in industrial supplies and equipment.

These vendors are known to report payment activity to bureaus like Dun & Bradstreet, Experian, and Equifax.

Step 2: Apply for Vendor Accounts

Once you've identified suitable vendors, apply for accounts with them. Here's what you'll need:

- A registered business with an EIN.
- A business bank account.
- Consistent business information across all documents (address, phone number, etc.).

Start with net-30 accounts, which require payment within 30 days of the invoice date. These terms are ideal for building a positive payment history.

Step 3: Use Vendor Accounts Regularly

Place small, manageable orders to ensure you can pay invoices on time or early. Regular use of vendor accounts shows consistent financial activity, which strengthens your credit profile.

Step 4: Monitor and Manage Payments

Keep track of payment deadlines to avoid late payments. Early payments not only improve your credit scores but also foster goodwill with vendors, which can lead to better terms.

TYPES OF TRADE LINES TO ESTABLISH

Diversifying your trade lines is one of the most effective strategies to build a robust and resilient credit profile. Think of your trade lines as the different tools in a financial toolkit—each serving a unique purpose and contributing to the overall strength of your business's financial standing. A variety of trade lines not only enhances your creditworthiness but also prepares your business to handle diverse financial scenarios. Below, let's explore the main types of trade lines and how they can add value to your business.

Vendor Trade Lines

Vendor trade lines are credit accounts with suppliers that offer payment terms such as net-30, net-60, or net-90. These terms mean that payment is due 30, 60, or 90 days after the invoice date, providing you with additional time to manage cash flow. Vendor trade lines are often the first and easiest type of credit to establish for new businesses. Examples include:

- **Office Supply Companies:** Vendors like Quill and Staples supply essential business items while helping you build your payment history.

- **Wholesale Distributors:** These companies provide bulk inventory or supplies crucial for day-to-day operations.

- **Service Providers:** Utilities, internet services, and logistics companies are also common sources of vendor trade lines.

By maintaining consistent payments with these vendors, your business can build a solid credit foundation while improving relationships that may lead to better terms over time.

Retail Trade Lines

Retail trade lines are accounts with major retailers that extend credit to businesses. These accounts are particularly beneficial for purchasing operational supplies, equipment, or other necessities. Common examples include:

- **Amazon Business:** Ideal for a wide range of supplies, from office essentials to specialized equipment.

- **Staples:** Offers credit accounts specifically tailored for business customers purchasing office supplies.

- **Lowe's or Home Depot:** Perfect for businesses in construction or renovation, offering materials and tools on credit.

Retail trade lines not only support operational needs but also help diversify your credit profile, demonstrating your ability to manage multiple credit relationships effectively.

Revolving Credit Lines

Revolving credit accounts, such as business credit cards, provide flexibility for ongoing expenses. These accounts allow you to borrow up to a specified limit and repay as needed, with the option to reuse the credit as you pay down balances. Benefits include:

- **Flexibility:** You can use revolving credit to cover unexpected expenses or short-term operational costs.

- **Credit Management:** Proper use demonstrates your ability to manage ongoing credit responsibly.

- **Rewards Programs:** Many business credit cards offer cashback or travel rewards, adding value to your spending.

Examples include cards like the Capital One Spark for Business or American Express Blue Business Cash.

Installment Trade Lines

Installment loans, such as equipment financing, vehicle loans, or term loans, are another critical type of trade line. These loans are paid back in fixed monthly installments over a specified period, making them excellent for demonstrating your ability to manage larger, long-term financial commitments. Examples include:

- **Equipment Financing:** For purchasing machinery, technology, or tools essential to your operations.

- **Vehicle Loans:** For acquiring company vehicles used in daily operations or logistics.

- **Term Loans:** For significant investments, such as expansions or facility upgrades.

These trade lines add diversity to your credit profile and reflect your capacity to handle substantial financial responsibilities over time.

BEST PRACTICES FOR MANAGING TRADE LINES

Effectively managing trade lines is just as important as establishing them. Imagine each trade line as a thread in the financial fabric of your business—when woven together with care, they create a strong, resilient structure that can withstand the challenges of growth and market fluctuations. Proper management not only ensures that these trade lines continue to work in your favor but also enhances your reputation with vendors and credit bureaus. Here's how to make the most of your accounts:

Pay Invoices Early

Whenever possible, pay invoices before the due date to showcase your financial discipline. Early payments do more than meet expectations—they create trust with your vendors, improve your Dun & Bradstreet PAYDEX score, and can often lead to better terms, such as extended payment periods or increased credit limits. Vendors tend to prioritize businesses with a proven track record of prompt payments, making this a simple yet powerful strategy for long-term success.

Monitor Account Activity

Regularly review your account activity to ensure every payment is recorded accurately by your vendors and the credit bureaus. Mistakes, such as unreported payments or errors in billing, can harm your credit profile if left unaddressed. Develop a routine to audit your statements and cross-check payments against vendor records. Promptly addressing discrepancies not only protects your credit scores but also signals to vendors that you are meticulous and reliable.

Communicate with Vendors

Shameka Landers

Proactive communication is key to maintaining strong vendor relationships. If you foresee challenges in meeting a payment deadline, inform your vendors early and discuss potential solutions. Many vendors appreciate transparency and may offer temporary adjustments, such as extended deadlines or partial payment options, to avoid reporting late payments to credit bureaus. Open, honest dialogue fosters trust and can help you weather financial hiccups without damaging your credit profile.

Limit Credit Utilization

High credit utilization—using a significant portion of your available credit—can signal financial strain to lenders and negatively impact your credit scores. Aim to keep your credit utilization rate below 30%, even during busy periods. For example, if you have $50,000 in available credit, try not to exceed $15,000 in usage. Balancing your utilization demonstrates financial stability and ensures you have enough credit available for unexpected needs.

Keep Records Organized

Detailed records are your best defense against disputes or misunderstandings. Maintain organized files for all trade line transactions, including invoices, payment confirmations, and correspondence with vendors. Digital tools like accounting software or cloud-based systems can simplify record-keeping, ensuring quick access to critical documents when needed. These records not only support credit disputes but also serve as a valuable resource for analyzing spending patterns and optimizing vendor relationships.

Shameka Landers

THE LONG-TERM BENEFITS OF TRADE LINES

Building and maintaining trade lines is an investment in your business's future. Over time, you'll reap the following rewards:

- **Stronger Credit Scores:** A consistent history of positive payment activity builds a robust credit profile, showcasing your business's financial responsibility. This strong profile opens doors to better financing opportunities and favorable terms.

- **Access to Capital:** Reliable trade line relationships can lead to higher credit limits, increased purchasing power, and better loan options. This access to capital enables your business to grow, expand operations, or invest in new ventures without straining cash flow.

- **Increased Credibility:** Vendors, lenders, and even potential partners view businesses with established and well-maintained trade lines as dependable and professional. This credibility enhances your reputation and fosters trust within your industry.

- **Financial Flexibility:** Trade lines provide the breathing room needed to navigate unpredictable cash flow cycles, invest in growth initiatives, or manage unforeseen expenses. This flexibility ensures your business remains resilient during both opportunities and challenges.

- **Stronger Negotiation Power:** Businesses with a solid credit history and reliable trade line usage often find themselves in a stronger position to negotiate better payment terms, discounts, or extended credit periods with vendors.

- **Improved Vendor Relationships:** Positive trade line management builds long-term trust with vendors, which can lead to exclusive deals, loyalty rewards, and more personalized service—all of which contribute to operational efficiency and cost savings.

- **Preparation for Economic Downturns:** A strong trade line foundation acts as a financial cushion during economic uncertainties, providing your business with stability and the resources needed to adapt to changing market conditions.

By leveraging these benefits, trade lines not only serve your immediate operational needs but also position your business for sustainable success in the long run.

Building trade lines and vendor accounts is a fundamental step in establishing and strengthening your business credit. By carefully selecting vendors, maintaining positive payment histories, and diversifying your credit profile, you're not just improving your scores—you're laying the groundwork for sustainable growth and success. In the next chapter, we'll explore how to leverage your established credit to secure loans and financing that fuel your business ambitions.

5

LEVERAGING BUSINESS CREDIT FOR GROWTH

Capital is the lifeblood of a growing business

Establishing a strong credit profile is a significant milestone, but it's only the beginning of a much larger journey. Picture this: you've built a solid foundation for your business, and now, with the power of business credit, you have a key that opens doors to opportunities that seemed out of reach. Whether it's scaling operations, launching new ventures, or weathering unforeseen challenges, business credit is your gateway to growth. More than just a safety net, it's a dynamic tool that can reshape the way your business operates, thrives, and competes in today's marketplace. In this chapter, we explore how to harness the potential of business credit strategically, empowering you to expand your horizons, invest in innovation, and secure a prosperous future for your company.

Shameka Landers

UNDERSTANDING THE POWER OF BUSINESS CREDIT

Business credit is more than a financial tool; it's a gateway to resources that can transform your business. By tapping into your established credit, you can:

- **Expand Operations:** Open new locations, scale production, or increase your service offerings. Business credit allows you to take calculated risks, ensuring that expansion is sustainable and aligned with market demands.

- **Invest in Technology:** Upgrade equipment, adopt innovative tools, or integrate advanced systems that enhance efficiency. Technology investments often provide long-term cost savings and operational improvements that keep your business competitive.

- **Hire Talent:** Attract skilled professionals who can drive your business forward. Business credit enables you to onboard top talent without immediate financial strain, allowing for strategic hires that support growth.

- **Strengthen Cash Flow:** Cover operational costs during slow periods or fund large projects without depleting reserves. Strong cash flow management ensures stability during market fluctuations.

- **Boost Marketing Efforts:** Allocate funds toward advertising campaigns, SEO, and social media strategies to expand your reach and increase sales. Effective marketing drives revenue and enhances brand recognition.

- **Build Inventory:** Use credit to purchase inventory in bulk at lower costs, ensuring that you meet customer demand during peak seasons. Adequate stock levels reduce missed sales opportunities.

- **Enhance Customer Experience:** Invest in customer-facing upgrades such as point-of-sale systems, loyalty programs, or customer service training to increase satisfaction and retention.

- **Fund Research and Development:** Use credit to explore new product lines, test prototypes, or conduct market research. Innovation ensures your business remains relevant and adaptable to changing consumer preferences.

TYPES OF FINANCING TO LEVERAGE

Using business credit effectively begins with understanding the types of financing available and how they align with your goals. Each option serves a unique purpose and caters to different business needs, making it essential to evaluate your priorities before proceeding:

1. Business Credit Cards

Business credit cards are a versatile tool for managing everyday expenses. Their benefits include:

- **Rewards Programs:** Earn cashback, travel points, or discounts on essential purchases like office supplies and travel.

- **Expense Tracking:** Simplify bookkeeping by categorizing transactions automatically, saving time and ensuring accuracy.

- **Revolving Credit:** Access funds quickly for unforeseen expenses or operational needs without reapplying for loans.

When using business credit cards, prioritize responsible usage by keeping balances low and paying off monthly statements in full to avoid high-interest charges.

2. Business Lines of Credit

A business line of credit provides revolving access to funds, making it an ideal solution for businesses that experience fluctuating cash flow. Key advantages include:

- **Flexibility:** Withdraw only the amount you need and pay interest solely on what you use.

- **Seasonal Support:** Manage costs during off-peak times or ramp up production during busy seasons.

- **Quick Access:** Ideal for short-term projects or unexpected opportunities.

3. Term Loans

Term loans offer a lump sum of capital upfront, repaid over a fixed period with interest. These loans are particularly effective for:

- **Large Investments:** Purchase high-value assets like real estate or heavy machinery.

- **Business Expansion:** Open new locations or invest in infrastructure upgrades.

- **Predictable Repayments:** Fixed monthly payments make budgeting straightforward.

4. Equipment Financing

Designed specifically for purchasing essential tools and machinery, equipment financing is a practical choice for businesses reliant on specialized equipment. Features include:

- **Lower Risk:** The equipment itself acts as collateral, reducing the lender's risk and making approval easier.

- **Cost Efficiency:** Spread the cost of expensive assets over time without depleting reserves.

- **Operational Upgrades:** Improve productivity by investing in modern, efficient technology.

5. Invoice Financing

Invoice financing is a lifeline for businesses with lengthy payment cycles. By borrowing against unpaid invoices, you can:

- **Boost Cash Flow:** Receive immediate funds instead of waiting 30, 60, or 90 days for clients to pay.

- **Ease Operational Stress:** Maintain smooth operations without financial disruptions.

- **Bridge Gaps:** Cover payroll, utilities, or inventory purchases while awaiting payments.

6. Revenue-Based Financing

This option allows you to borrow funds based on your business's projected revenue. It's an attractive choice for growing companies with consistent cash flow but minimal assets. Benefits include:

- **Flexible Repayments:** Payments are tied to revenue, scaling up or down depending on income.

- **No Collateral Required:** Approval is based on revenue rather than asset value.

- **Fast Funding:** Ideal for businesses needing capital quickly to seize opportunities.

7. Merchant Cash Advances

Merchant cash advances provide upfront funding in exchange for a percentage of future credit card sales. While often expensive, they can be useful for businesses with high-volume transactions, offering:

- **Immediate Access:** Funds are available quickly, helping meet urgent financial needs.

- **No Fixed Payments:** Repayments are proportional to sales, easing the burden during slower periods.

- **Minimal Paperwork:** Approval is based on sales history rather than detailed financial documentation.

Each of these financing options offers distinct advantages, allowing businesses to select the most suitable solution based on their specific goals and operational challenges. The key to leveraging these tools lies in aligning them with your business's immediate and long-term needs.

STRATEGIES FOR LEVERAGING CREDIT WISELY

To make the most of your business credit, adopt the following strategies:

1. Align Financing with Goals

Before applying for credit, clearly define your business goals. Whether you're expanding operations, investing in new products, or improving cash flow, choose financing options that align with your objectives.

2. Avoid Over-Leveraging

Borrowing beyond your means can lead to financial strain and damage your credit profile. Conduct a thorough assessment of your repayment capacity before taking on new debt.

3. Diversify Credit Sources

Relying on a single type of credit can limit your options and increase risk. Maintain a mix of credit cards, vendor accounts, and loans to create a well-rounded credit profile.

4. Monitor Credit Usage

Keep your credit utilization rate below 30% to maintain a strong credit score. Regularly review your accounts to ensure you're staying within healthy limits.

5. Build Relationships with Lenders

Strong relationships with lenders can lead to better terms, higher credit limits, and quicker approvals. Communicate openly and consistently to foster trust.

Shameka Landers

6. Use Credit for Revenue-Generating Activities

Leverage credit for investments that directly contribute to revenue growth, such as marketing campaigns, product launches, or facility upgrades.

REAL-LIFE CASE STUDIES

Learning from the experiences of other businesses can provide valuable insights. Here are two examples of companies that successfully leveraged business credit:

Case Study 1: Expanding a Retail Chain

A small retail chain in the Midwest faced increasing customer demand but lacked the capital to expand its operations. After consulting with a financial advisor, they utilized a combination of term loans and vendor trade lines to open three new locations. The term loans provided the upfront funds necessary for real estate, renovations, and equipment, while the vendor trade lines enabled them to stock inventory without immediate out-of-pocket costs. By diligently managing their credit, maintaining strong payment histories, and cultivating relationships with lenders, the business gained access to additional credit facilities. Within two years, their annual revenue grew by 40%, and their expanded footprint allowed them to negotiate bulk purchasing discounts, further improving profitability.

Case Study 2: Investing in Technology

A mid-sized manufacturing company identified outdated machinery as a bottleneck to scaling their production. To address this, they secured equipment financing through a specialized lender. The financing terms allowed them to purchase cutting-edge production equipment without depleting their cash reserves. The improved efficiency reduced operational costs by 25% and doubled their production capacity, enabling them to meet growing customer demands. The company reinvested the savings into marketing and distribution efforts, launching a successful campaign that increased brand visibility and captured new markets. Over the course of three years, the investment in technology not only strengthened their bottom line but also positioned them as a leader in their industry.

THE RISKS OF MISMANAGING BUSINESS CREDIT

While business credit is a powerful tool, it must be used responsibly. Common pitfalls to avoid include:

- **Over-Leveraging:** Taking on too much debt can lead to cash flow issues and jeopardize your financial stability. Over-leveraging may also limit your ability to access future credit, as lenders become wary of extending additional financing to heavily indebted businesses.

- **Neglecting Payments:** Late payments harm your credit score and damage relationships with lenders and vendors. They may also result in late fees, increased interest rates, or loss of favorable terms that were previously negotiated.

- **Ignoring Terms:** Failing to understand loan terms can result in unexpected fees or unfavorable conditions. For example, missing clauses about prepayment penalties or variable interest rates can lead to financial surprises that strain your business resources.

- **Failing to Monitor Credit Reports:** Neglecting regular checks of your business credit reports can allow errors or fraudulent activities to go unnoticed. These discrepancies can negatively impact your creditworthiness if not addressed promptly.

- **Mixing Personal and Business Finances:** Using personal credit for business expenses creates financial entanglements that can hurt both your personal and business credit profiles. It also complicates financial reporting and tax preparation.

- **Relying Too Heavily on One Source of Credit:** Depending solely on one type of credit, such as business credit cards, limits your financial flexibility and increases risk if that source becomes unavailable.

- **Failing to Plan for Repayments:** Borrowing without a clear repayment plan can quickly lead to missed payments or default. A lack of structured repayment strategies puts your credit profile and relationships with lenders at risk.

Leveraging business credit is an essential part of growing your company. By understanding the types of financing available, aligning credit usage with your goals, and adopting responsible strategies, you can unlock new opportunities and achieve sustainable growth. In the next chapter, we'll explore advanced credit management techniques to help you maintain and protect your credit profile as your business evolves.

Shameka Landers

6

SCALING YOUR BUSINESS WITH BUSINESS CREDIT

Growth is never by mere chance; it is the result of forces working together

Every thriving business reaches a point where the question isn't whether to grow, but how to do so effectively. Growth is a thrilling milestone—a testament to your vision, hard work, and determination. Yet, it also brings its own set of challenges: how do you fund expansion without overstretching your resources? How do you maintain a steady cash flow while scaling operations? And most importantly, how do you ensure that growth is sustainable and doesn't jeopardize the stability of your business?

This is where business credit comes in as a transformative force. It's more than just a financial resource; it's a strategic tool that, when used wisely, can unlock new opportunities and fuel the next phase of your journey. In this chapter, we'll dive deep into the ways you can leverage business credit to fund critical growth initiatives, balance debt effectively, and set your business up for long-term success. By understanding the potential of business credit and applying it strategically, you'll gain the confidence to navigate the challenges of scaling while reaping its rewards.

STRATEGIC USE OF BUSINESS CREDIT

Scaling a business requires strategic planning, and business credit is one of the most effective tools at your disposal. Here are some key ways to use credit strategically:

1. Fund Inventory Purchases

As your business grows, demand for your products or services may increase. Business credit can help you purchase inventory in bulk, allowing you to:

- **Save Money:** Leverage bulk purchasing discounts.

- **Ensure Readiness:** Stock up during peak seasons to meet customer demand.

- **Avoid Cash Flow Issues:** Pay for inventory on credit while revenue from sales covers operational costs.

2. Hire and Retain Top Talent

Hiring skilled employees is critical for growth, but onboarding and training can strain resources. Business credit provides the flexibility to:

- Offer competitive salaries.

- Invest in training and professional development.

- Expand your workforce as operations grow.

Shameka Landers

3. Expand to New Locations

Whether opening a second storefront or launching in a new market, growth often requires physical expansion. Business credit can fund:

- Real estate leases or purchases.
- Renovations and equipment for new facilities.
- Marketing campaigns to attract customers in new areas.

4. Invest in Technology

Technology is a growth catalyst. Use business credit to invest in tools and systems that improve efficiency, such as:

- Point-of-sale (POS) systems for retail businesses.
- Customer relationship management (CRM) software.
- Automated solutions for logistics and supply chain management.

5. Boost Marketing and Branding Efforts

To scale effectively, your brand needs visibility. Business credit allows you to:

- Launch multi-channel marketing campaigns.
- Improve your online presence through SEO and digital advertising.
- Rebrand or update your company's image to appeal to broader audiences.

6. Balance Debt and Cash Flow

Scaling often involves taking on new financial commitments. Business credit helps you:

- Manage operational costs while waiting for revenue to increase.

- Avoid disruptions to daily operations.

- Consolidate smaller debts into manageable monthly payments.

TIPS FOR SUSTAINABLE GROWTH USING BUSINESS CREDIT

Scaling with credit is a balancing act that requires thoughtful planning and strategic execution. Here are detailed tips to ensure sustainable growth:

1. Set Clear Growth Goals

Define what growth means for your business in both the short and long term. Are you expanding into new geographical regions, launching a new product line, increasing market share, or improving operational efficiency? Specific and measurable goals will help you align your credit usage with your overall strategy, ensuring you don't overextend resources while scaling effectively.

2. Create a Detailed Budget

A well-structured budget is the backbone of sustainable scaling. Break down costs into categories such as marketing, inventory, staffing, technology upgrades, and infrastructure expansion. Factor in both fixed and variable costs and identify areas where business credit can provide support. This detailed approach helps determine how much credit you need, ensuring funds are allocated efficiently without unnecessary borrowing.

3. Monitor Financial Metrics

Track critical financial metrics, including revenue growth, profit margins, cash flow, and customer acquisition costs. These metrics provide valuable insights into the health of your scaling efforts. For example, if profit margins decrease, you can adjust credit allocations to prioritize high-return activities. Regular monitoring allows you to pivot strategies quickly and make data-driven decisions.

4. Build Strong Vendor Relationships

Vendors that trust your business are more likely to offer favorable terms, such as extended payment cycles, flexible credit limits, or bulk purchasing discounts. Strengthening these relationships through consistent communication and timely payments enhances your business's reputation, leading to long-term benefits and smoother scaling efforts.

5. Diversify Revenue Streams

Relying on a single product, service, or market increases vulnerability. Use business credit strategically to explore new revenue streams. This could include expanding your product offerings, targeting a new customer demographic, or entering a different market sector. Diversification reduces risk and creates additional pathways for growth.

6. Pay Down Balances Early When Possible

Early repayment of credit balances reduces interest costs and strengthens your business credit profile. A strong profile not only improves your creditworthiness but also makes it easier to access additional funding on better terms in the future. Prioritize paying down high-interest debts first to maximize savings.

7. Invest in Scalable Technology

Use credit to adopt technology that supports scaling efforts, such as automation tools, advanced data analytics, or cloud-based systems. These technologies improve efficiency, reduce operational costs, and prepare your business for sustained growth.

8. Maintain Adequate Cash Reserves

While credit is a valuable tool, it's essential to maintain cash reserves for unexpected expenses or economic downturns. A healthy cash reserve acts as a safety net, ensuring you can navigate challenges without relying solely on borrowed funds.

By following these strategies, you can use business credit as a powerful catalyst for sustainable and impactful growth, ensuring your business scales efficiently and remains resilient in the face of challenges.

BALANCING DEBT AND RISK

Using business credit can open many doors for growth, but it's important to approach it with care. Here are some practical strategies to help you manage the risks that come with borrowing:

Borrow Responsibly:

Only take on the debt you truly need. Borrowing too much can put a strain on your cash flow, making it harder to stay flexible when unexpected challenges arise.

Keep a Financial Safety Net:

Always have some cash set aside for emergencies. Whether it's a sudden repair, unexpected legal fees, or a slowdown in business, a solid reserve can help you avoid the pitfalls of relying too heavily on credit.

Understand Your Loan Terms:

Before signing any credit agreement, make sure you know exactly what you're getting into. Pay close attention to interest rates, fees, repayment schedules, and any hidden clauses—like penalties for early repayment or variable interest rates—that could impact your long-term financial plans.

Plan Your Repayments:

Develop a clear strategy for paying back your debt. Consider setting up automated payments or focusing on paying off loans with higher interest rates first. This approach can help you keep overall costs down and prevent any surprises down the road.

Monitor Your Credit Use:

Try to keep your credit utilization below 30% of your total available credit. Keeping your borrowing in check not only protects your credit score but also reassures lenders that your business is financially healthy.

Diversify Your Credit Sources:

Shameka Landers

Don't put all your eggs in one basket. A mix of vendor accounts, business credit cards, and term loans can provide the flexibility you need and offer a buffer if one type of credit becomes problematic.

Educate Your Team:

If others in your company are involved in financial decision-making, make sure they understand the importance of responsible credit use. Mismanagement by even one team member can lead to unnecessary expenses or missed payments, which might harm your overall credit profile.

While business credit is a powerful tool for funding everything from inventory to new hires and technology upgrades, it requires thoughtful planning and discipline. In our next chapter, we'll delve into some common mistakes in managing business credit and discuss effective ways to overcome these challenges.

7

MANAGING DEBT AND AVOIDING COMMON PITFALLS

> *"Debt is like fire: if controlled, it can be a useful tool; if left unchecked, it can destroy everything in its path."*

Debt can be both a powerful tool and a dangerous trap. When used wisely, it can drive your business' growth, fuel your expansion, and provide the financial flexibility that you need to navigate challenges. However, if mismanaged, debt can quickly become an overwhelming burden that stifles progress and even threatens the survival of your business.

Managing business credit isn't merely about crossing numbers; it's about making sound financial choices that support your business for the long run. Every successful entrepreneur who has achieved success understands that debt should serve as a stepping stone to new opportunities—not a stumbling block that impedes progress.

Shameka Landers

COMMON CREDIT MANAGEMENT MISTAKES

Managing business credit effectively is a very crucial part of running a successful enterprise. Many business owners unknowingly make financial missteps due to a lack of information or a short-term mindset. Avoiding these pitfalls can mean the difference between long-term financial stability and unnecessary debt.

1. Mixing Personal and Business Finances

One of the most common mistakes entrepreneurs make is using personal credit for business expenses or vice versa. While this may seem convenient, it can lead to financial confusion and even legal issues down the road.

Why This is a Problem:

- Blurs the line between personal and business liabilities, putting personal assets at risk.

- Makes it harder to build a strong business credit profile.

- Complicates tax reporting and deductions.

- Lenders may be hesitant to extend business credit if personal and business finances are intertwined.

- Increases the risk of accumulating debt without clear financial oversight.

- Compromises legal and financial protection in case of business disputes or liability issues.

How to Avoid This Mistake:

- Open a dedicated business bank account and use it exclusively for company transactions.

- Apply for business credit cards instead of using personal ones.

- Maintain detailed financial records to ensure clear separation between personal and business expenses.

- Work with a financial advisor to develop an effective credit management strategy.

- Properly register your business to establish a clear legal distinction from personal finances.

A business without financial boundaries is like a house without walls—it won't stand for long. Keeping personal and business finances separate is essential to safeguarding your financial future.

2. Over-Leveraging Credit

Using credit to support business growth is common, but relying too heavily on borrowed funds can create long-term financial instability.

Why This is a Problem:

- High debt levels can strain cash flow and limit future borrowing capacity.

- Increases the risk of default, negatively affecting business credit scores.

- Makes a business vulnerable to economic downturns.

- Lenders may hesitate to extend further credit to businesses with excessive outstanding debt.

- Rapid expansion without financial stability can lead to closure instead of growth.

- Interest payments on excessive debt can eat into profit margins, reducing opportunities for reinvestment.

How to Avoid This Mistake:

- Borrow only what your business can reasonably repay within a set timeframe.

- Monitor your credit utilization rate, keeping it below 30% of your available credit.

- Diversify financing sources, such as trade credit, business lines of credit, and revenue-based funding.

- Conduct regular financial health assessments to ensure debt levels remain manageable.

- Develop a structured debt repayment plan before taking on additional credit obligations.

Borrow wisely—your ability to manage today's obligations will determine your business's financial future.

3. Failing to Review Credit Reports

Many business owners assume their credit reports are accurate, but errors and fraudulent activity are more common than people realize. Overlooking these issues can cost a business valuable opportunities.

Why This is a Problem:

- Incorrect negative reports can lower your credit score and affect loan approvals.

- Fraudulent accounts or unauthorized transactions can go unnoticed.

- Business owners may miss opportunities to dispute and correct errors.

- Lenders and vendors rely on credit reports to determine your business's reliability.

- Old or incorrect data can linger and impact future business credit decisions.

- Lack of credit monitoring may result in undetected fraudulent activity.

How to Avoid This Mistake:

- Regularly check credit reports from major business credit bureaus (Dun & Bradstreet, Experian, Equifax).

- Set up credit monitoring alerts to track any changes in real time.

- Dispute any errors promptly and provide the necessary documentation for corrections.

- Stay proactive in reviewing and updating financial records.

Shameka Landers

- Assign a team member or financial advisor to oversee credit health and identify any irregularities.

Your business credit report is your financial reputation—protect it as carefully as you would your business itself.

Avoiding these common business credit mistakes is essential for long-term success. By keeping personal and business finances separate, borrowing responsibly, and staying on top of credit reports, you can maintain financial stability and ensure your business is positioned for growth. Managing credit wisely is not just about securing funding; it's about building a strong financial foundation for the future.

PROACTIVE CREDIT MANAGEMENT STRATEGIES

Rather than fixing mistakes after they occur, take proactive steps to ensure financial stability and credit health.

1. Establish a Business Emergency Fund

A cash reserve can prevent the need to rely on credit during slow periods or unexpected downturns.

How to build one:

- Allocate a percentage of **monthly revenue** to a separate emergency fund.

- Keep enough savings to cover **three to six months of expenses**.

- Consider a **business savings account** with high interest to grow your funds.

- Automate savings to ensure consistent contributions.

- Diversify the fund across multiple accounts or assets to increase security.

- Regularly review and adjust the fund based on business performance and risk factors.

An emergency fund isn't an expense—it's an insurance policy against financial instability.

2. Pay Off Debt Faster

The faster you pay off business debt, the less you spend on interest and fees.

Strategies to accelerate repayment:

- Make **biweekly payments** instead of monthly to reduce principal faster.

- Use windfalls, such as tax refunds or surplus revenue, to pay down debts.

- Refinance high-interest loans when better rates become available.

- Avoid minimum payments and strive to clear balances ahead of schedule.

- Negotiate lower interest rates with lenders to reduce long-term costs.

- Establish a structured debt snowball or avalanche method for repayment priorities.

- Seek professional financial advice on restructuring large or complicated debts.

Debt is a burden, but the speed at which you release it determines your financial freedom.

3. Diversify Credit Sources

Relying on a single type of credit can create vulnerabilities if financial conditions change. A diversified credit strategy can provide flexibility and financial resilience.

How to do it:

- Maintain **vendor trade lines** for inventory purchases.

- Use a **business line of credit** for short-term needs rather than credit cards.

- Explore **alternative financing**, such as revenue-based funding or grants.

- Establish relationships with multiple banks to ensure financing options remain open.

- Invest in building strong relationships with lenders who specialize in your industry.

- Consider angel investors or venture capital if looking for strategic financial partners.

- Seek partnerships with suppliers that offer extended payment terms.

A wise entrepreneur never depends on just one financial lifeline—diversification is the key to stability.

4. Strengthen Vendor and Supplier Relationships

Good credit management extends beyond lenders—it also includes vendors and suppliers who offer trade credit terms that can be invaluable for cash flow management.

Ways to strengthen these relationships:

- Make payments **ahead of schedule** to build trust and improve terms.

- Negotiate **longer payment cycles** to better align with your cash flow.

- Work with vendors who **report payments to credit bureaus** to build your business credit.

- Establish long-term contracts with reliable suppliers for stability.

- Communicate openly about financial challenges to explore flexible solutions.

- Seek volume-based discounts by consolidating purchases with preferred vendors.

Strong business relationships are the foundation of better credit terms and sustainable growth.

5. Monitor and Improve Business Credit Scores

A strong credit profile opens doors to better financing options and partnerships.

How to enhance your credit standing:

- Regularly review your business credit reports from **Dun & Bradstreet, Experian, and Equifax.**

- Address errors and discrepancies promptly through disputes.

- Keep credit utilization low to reflect strong financial management.

- Increase credit limits but avoid maxing out available credit.

- Maintain older credit accounts to establish long-term credit history.

- Ensure that all financial commitments are met on time.

- Use credit-building tools such as secured business loans and net-30 accounts.

Your credit score isn't just a number—it's your financial passport to business growth.

KEY TAKEAWAYS

- **Avoid common pitfalls** such as over-leveraging, neglecting credit reports, and mixing personal finances with business expenses.

- **Have a repayment plan** in place before taking on debt to ensure long-term financial health.

- **Recover from mistakes** by negotiating better terms, disputing credit errors, and improving financial management.

- **Be proactive** by building emergency funds, diversifying credit sources, and using disciplined repayment strategies.

- **Keep credit under control** by balancing borrowing with sustainable revenue streams and operational efficiency.

- **Educate your team** on financial literacy and responsible credit usage to foster long-term stability.

By following these strategies, you can **use business credit as a powerful tool for growth rather than a financial burden**. Smart debt management is the foundation of long-term business success, ensuring you stay financially resilient in any market condition.

8

SMART FINANCIAL MANAGEMENT

"Financial management is not about getting rich quickly; it's about ensuring sustainability, growth, and resilience in any economic climate."

Effective financial management is the backbone of any successful business. It is what separates thriving businesses from those that struggle to stay afloat. Managing business finances wisely means ensuring steady cash flow, making informed borrowing decisions, optimizing costs, and investing strategically in business growth.

This chapter will guide you through the key financial strategies every entrepreneur needs to master, focusing on budgeting, cash flow management, debt management, and long-term financial planning.

1. The Importance of Budgeting in Business

Budgeting is more than just keeping track of numbers; it's about setting clear financial goals and ensuring your business has the resources needed to achieve them. A well-structured budget gives business owners control over their finances, prevents unnecessary spending, and allows for strategic reinvestment.

How to Create an Effective Business Budget:

- **Define Your Revenue Streams** – Identify all sources of income, including product sales, service revenue, and any external funding.

- **Categorize Expenses** – Differentiate between fixed costs (rent, utilities, salaries) and variable costs (marketing, materials, transportation).

- **Set Profitability Goals** – Determine how much revenue must exceed expenses for sustainable growth.

- **Allocate a Contingency Fund** – Set aside 5-10% of your revenue for unexpected expenses or downturns.

- **Review and Adjust Monthly** – A budget should not be static. Adjust projections based on actual business performance.

- **Use Financial Software** – Tools like QuickBooks, Xero, or FreshBooks can help automate and analyze budgeting effectively.

A business without a budget is like driving with your eyes closed. You need to see where your money is going.

2. Cash Flow Management: The Lifeblood of Your Business

Cash flow is the movement of money in and out of your business. Even a profitable business can fail if it runs out of cash. Managing cash flow effectively ensures that a business can cover expenses, invest in growth, and stay financially healthy.

Best Practices for Cash Flow Management:

1. **Maintain a Cash Flow Forecast** – Predict upcoming expenses and income to avoid shortages.

2. **Invoice Promptly and Follow Up on Payments** – Delayed payments can choke cash flow. Set clear payment terms and automate reminders.

3. **Negotiate Favorable Payment Terms** – Extend vendor payment deadlines while encouraging customers to pay faster.

4. **Optimize Inventory Management** – Overstocking ties up cash unnecessarily, while understocking can lead to lost sales.

5. **Reduce Unnecessary Expenses** – Identify non-essential costs and minimize wastage.

6. **Use a Business Line of Credit** – A line of credit can help bridge short-term cash flow gaps.

7. **Diversify Revenue Streams** – Expanding your income sources reduces dependence on a single revenue channel.

Cash flow problems don't mean your business is failing, but failing to manage cash flow can lead to business failure.

3. Debt Management Strategies for Sustainable Growth

While credit can be a powerful tool for growth, excessive or mismanaged debt can cripple a business. Smart debt management involves ensuring that borrowing decisions align with financial goals.

How to Manage Business Debt Wisely:

- **Prioritize High-Interest Debt** – Pay off loans with the highest interest rates first to reduce overall costs.

- **Use Debt for Growth, Not Survival** – Borrowing should fund expansions and revenue-generating activities, not operational shortfalls.

- **Refinance When Possible** – Consider restructuring loans for lower interest rates or better repayment terms.

- **Monitor Debt-to-Income Ratio** – Keep debt manageable in relation to revenue.

- **Limit Credit Card Reliance** – Business credit cards are useful but should not replace structured financing solutions.

- **Ensure On-Time Payments** – Late payments impact credit scores and lender trust.

- **Consult Financial Experts** – Seeking professional advice can prevent costly financial mistakes.

Debt should be a tool, not a trap. Use it to build, not to bury your business.

4. Cost Optimization: Maximizing Efficiency Without Cutting Corners

Smart financial management means making the most of every dollar without compromising quality. Cost optimization strategies help businesses operate efficiently while maintaining profitability.

Ways to Optimize Costs Without Compromising Quality:

- **Automate Routine Tasks** – Investing in software can save time and reduce labor costs.

- **Negotiate Supplier Contracts** – Strong vendor relationships can lead to bulk discounts and better payment terms.

- **Outsource Non-Core Activities** – Consider outsourcing tasks like bookkeeping, marketing, or IT support instead of hiring full-time staff.

- **Monitor Subscription Services** – Many businesses overpay for unused or unnecessary software subscriptions.

- **Encourage Remote Work** – Reducing office space expenses can significantly cut overhead costs.

- **Implement Energy-Efficient Practices** – Lowering utility costs benefits both the business and the environment.

Shameka Landers

- **Invest in Employee Training** – Skilled employees improve productivity and reduce costly mistakes.

Saving money is not about cutting corners—it's about making smarter financial choices.

5. Long-Term Financial Planning for Business Success

A well-thought-out financial plan is essential for business longevity. It ensures that companies are prepared for economic fluctuations and can take advantage of future opportunities.

Key Elements of a Strong Financial Plan:

1. **Define Long-Term Business Goals** – Set 5-10 year financial objectives for expansion, investment, and profitability.

2. **Create an Investment Strategy** – Reinvest profits in technology, personnel, or market expansion.

3. **Build a Strong Credit Profile** – A good credit history opens doors to better financing options.

4. **Plan for Economic Downturns** – Establish reserves and contingency plans for recessions or industry shifts.

5. **Evaluate Financial Risks Regularly** – Identify and mitigate risks related to market changes, competition, or operational inefficiencies.

6. **Ensure Retirement & Succession Planning** – Plan for business transition, whether through sale, succession, or closure.

7. **Regularly Review and Update Financial Strategies** – Adapt financial planning based on evolving market trends and business performance.

The best time to plan for the future is today. Financial preparedness ensures business survival and growth.

KEY TAKEAWAYS

- **Budgeting is essential** for tracking revenue, expenses, and financial goals.

- **Cash flow management** prevents business disruptions and ensures liquidity.

- **Debt should be managed wisely** to support growth, not hinder operations.

- **Cost optimization strategies** improve efficiency while maintaining quality.

- **Long-term financial planning** secures the future of the business.

By implementing these financial management strategies, business owners can navigate economic challenges, seize growth opportunities, and build a company that thrives for years to come.

THE FUTURE OF BUSINESS CREDIT

"The future of business credit isn't just about borrowing; it's about building financial agility and leveraging technology for smarter decision-making."

The landscape of business credit is evolving rapidly, driven by financial technology, new lending models, and changing economic conditions. Businesses that stay ahead of these trends will have a competitive edge, accessing better credit opportunities, reducing borrowing costs, and increasing financial flexibility.

This chapter is all about the future of business credit, emerging lending technologies, the role of AI in financial decision-making, and how businesses can prepare for upcoming changes in the credit landscape.

Shameka Landers

HOW BUSINESS CREDIT IS EVOLVING

Traditional business credit models relied on financial statements, collateral, and personal credit scores. While these factors are still relevant, the future of business credit is shifting towards:

- **Alternative Credit Scoring** – Fintech companies use machine learning to assess creditworthiness based on cash flow, transaction history, and industry trends rather than just financial statements. This allows businesses with limited credit history to secure funding based on their financial activity rather than traditional lending criteria.

- **Faster Approvals** – Automated underwriting speeds up loan approvals, reducing paperwork and manual verification. This results in quicker access to funds, which is crucial for businesses that require immediate financial assistance for expansion or operational needs.

- **More Flexible Credit Options** – Business credit is becoming more tailored, with lines of credit that adjust based on seasonal revenue fluctuations. Companies can access dynamic lending solutions that align with their revenue cycles, reducing the burden of fixed repayments during slow periods.

- **Blockchain-Based Lending** – Secure and transparent lending transactions using blockchain technology are gaining traction. Smart contracts streamline loan agreements, eliminating unnecessary intermediaries and reducing costs while ensuring greater security and compliance.

- **Expanded Access to Credit** – Businesses with limited credit history can access financing through non-traditional lenders who analyze real-time financial data. Lenders are increasingly considering alternative factors such as customer reviews, supply chain relationships, and operational efficiencies to determine creditworthiness.

- **Decentralized Finance (DeFi) Impact** – DeFi lending platforms are providing new opportunities for businesses to obtain financing through peer-to-peer networks, enabling direct lending without traditional banking institutions.

- **Integrated Credit Systems** – Many businesses are now leveraging embedded credit solutions within financial management platforms, allowing them to access credit seamlessly within their accounting software or payment processors.

Traditional credit scoring is being disrupted—future lending decisions will be data-driven and predictive.

EMERGING FINANCIAL TECHNOLOGIES SHAPING BUSINESS CREDIT

Technology is now changing how businesses access and manage credit. From AI-powered lending models to blockchain-driven security, financial innovation is making borrowing easier, safer, and more efficient. If you can understand these advancements, it will help you make better financial decisions and stay ahead of the competition.

How AI is Changing Business Lending

Artificial Intelligence (AI) is reshaping business credit by analyzing large set of data to make smarter lending decisions. This is done by:

- **Smarter Credit Scoring** – AI looks beyond traditional credit reports, assessing cash flow, supplier relationships, and market conditions to paint a more accurate picture of a company's financial health.

- **Stronger Fraud Detection** – AI-powered security systems spot unusual activity in loan applications, using biometric authentication and blockchain verification to prevent fraud.

- **Personalized Loan Offers** – AI-driven lenders use real-time financial data, e-commerce sales, and customer reviews to tailor loan options to individual businesses.

- **Better Risk Prediction** – AI identifies potential financial risks early, helping businesses and lenders make more informed decisions.

- **Instant Financial Guidance** – AI-powered chatbots and virtual assistants provide real-time insights to help businesses manage credit responsibly.

- **Flexible Interest Rates** – AI adjusts interest rates dynamically based on a company's financial performance, ensuring fairer lending terms.

Blockchain: A Game Changer for Business Credit

Blockchain technology is bringing more transparency, security, and efficiency to business lending. Here's how it's making a difference:

Shameka Landers

- **Smart Contracts** – Loan agreements can now be automated with smart contracts, eliminating the need for intermediaries and reducing paperwork.

- **Decentralized Credit Profiles** – Businesses gain more control over their financial data, allowing lenders to assess real-time creditworthiness without relying solely on credit bureaus.

- **Faster International Lending** – Blockchain removes barriers to global financing, reducing delays caused by currency conversion and regulatory hurdles.

- **Secure Transaction Records** – Every transaction is permanently recorded on a blockchain, reducing fraud risk and increasing trust between businesses and lenders.

- **New Ways to Secure Credit** – Tokenized credit assets could allow businesses to use blockchain-based financial instruments as collateral for funding.

- **Lower Loan Costs** – Automating loan processing through blockchain significantly cuts down administrative fees, making borrowing more affordable, especially for small businesses.

AI and blockchain are already changing business lending, making it more accessible, secure, and efficient. Companies that embrace these innovations will have a clear advantage, gaining faster access to funding, improved financial security, and smarter credit management. As technology continues to evolve, businesses that stay ahead of the curve will reap the greatest benefits.

Open Banking and Real-Time Data

Technology is now changing how businesses access credit, and open banking is at the forefront of this change. Because lenders can now securely access real-time financial data from business bank accounts, open banking is streamlining the borrowing process and providing businesses with greater financial flexibility. Here's how it's making an impact:

Faster Loan Approvals: Gone are the days of waiting weeks for loan approvals. With open banking, lenders can assess risk instantly, allowing businesses to secure credit approvals within minutes—without the hassle of submitting piles of paperwork.

Flexible Lending Terms: Every business experiences financial ups and downs. Open banking enables lenders to offer customized loan terms that adjust based on revenue fluctuations, ensuring businesses have access to credit when they need it most.

Improved Financial Insights: Having a clear view of your financial standing is crucial. Open banking gives businesses real-time insights into their credit profile and borrowing capacity, helping them make smarter financial decisions and optimize debt management.

Safe and Secure Data Sharing: Worried about data breaches? Open banking ensures that sensitive financial information is shared securely through advanced API integration, minimizing risks and keeping business data protected.

Seamless Accounting Integration: Managing finances becomes effortless when banking data syncs with accounting software. This integration allows for automated credit analysis, making financial tracking and forecasting more accurate and efficient.

Fair and Transparent Interest Rates: With access to real-time financial data, lenders can adjust interest rates based on a business's actual financial health. This means businesses with strong financial performance can benefit from lower, more competitive rates.

The Future of Business Credit: The financial landscape is evolving rapidly, and businesses that embrace open banking will have a competitive edge. By leveraging technology, companies can access smarter, faster, and more flexible credit options—ensuring they stay ahead in an increasingly digital world.

HOW YOUR BUSINESS CAN PREPARE FOR THE FUTURE OF CREDIT

To stay ahead, you must adopt strategies that enhance your financial resilience and creditworthiness.

1. Build a Strong Credit Profile

A strong credit profile is essential for your long-term financial stability. Establishing and maintaining good business credit can lead to better loan terms, higher credit limits, and lower interest rates.

- Maintain a low credit utilization ratio (below 30%) to show lenders you can manage credit responsibly.

- Ensure on-time payments to suppliers and lenders to avoid penalties and maintain a positive credit score.

- Monitor your business credit reports regularly and dispute inaccuracies to ensure your credit history reflects your actual financial behavior.

- Build credit history by using business credit accounts and making strategic purchases that you can pay off quickly.

- Strengthen relationships with credit agencies and lenders to improve your future borrowing opportunities.

- Educate your employees on proper financial management practices to avoid unnecessary debt accumulation.

A strong credit profile is like a safety net—it provides support when you need it most.

2. Embrace Financial Technology

Technology is reshaping the way you manage credit and financial planning. By leveraging the latest fintech tools, you can streamline your financial operations and make more informed borrowing decisions.

- Use fintech platforms to optimize cash flow and manage your credit lines efficiently.

- Automate financial reporting to improve loan approvals and reduce manual errors.

- Explore AI-driven financial tools for better budgeting and risk assessment, helping predict financial risks before they escalate.

- Implement cloud-based accounting software for real-time financial tracking and decision-making.

- Utilize digital payment platforms that integrate seamlessly with credit monitoring tools.

- Adopt cybersecurity measures to protect your sensitive financial data from fraud and breaches.

Technology is not just about speed; it's about making smarter, data-driven financial choices.

3. Diversify Your Credit Sources

Relying on a single source of credit can be risky, especially in uncertain economic conditions. Diversifying your credit sources ensures financial stability and greater borrowing flexibility.

- Combine traditional loans, revenue-based financing, and alternative lending models to reduce dependency on one credit source.

- Establish multiple credit relationships with banks, online lenders, and trade creditors to maximize your funding options.

- Negotiate longer repayment terms to improve liquidity and reduce financial strain.

- Leverage business credit cards with rewards and benefits that align with your business operations.

- Tap into government-backed loans and grants to supplement commercial financing options.

- Engage in networking with financial institutions to stay updated on new credit opportunities.

A diversified credit portfolio is like an investment strategy—balance is key to financial growth.

4. Prepare for Economic Fluctuations

Economic conditions are constantly shifting, and you must be prepared to adapt to these changes. Financial planning for downturns ensures stability during uncertain times.

- Create an emergency credit line for financial downturns to serve as a backup during cash flow shortages.

- Maintain a financial buffer to cover at least 6 months of expenses, allowing flexibility during crises.

- Develop contingency plans to adapt to market changes, including alternative revenue streams.

- Stay updated on economic trends and government regulations that may impact your business credit.

- Establish partnerships with investors or financial advisors to gain insights on economic forecasting.

- Invest in business insurance policies that protect against credit-related risks.

Success isn't about avoiding downturns—it's about preparing for them.

5. Strengthen Your Vendor and Banking Relationships

Strong relationships with financial institutions and vendors can unlock better credit terms and access to funding opportunities that might not be available to others.

- Build trust with financial institutions by maintaining transparency in your financial transactions and communication.

- Secure trade credit with suppliers to enhance financial flexibility and reduce upfront capital requirements.

- Use long-term banking partnerships to access exclusive credit opportunities, such as pre-approved loan offers.

- Negotiate lower interest rates and extended payment terms with key financial partners.

- Foster relationships with investors who can provide financial backing when needed.

- Regularly review credit agreements to ensure favorable terms are being maintained.

In business, relationships matter as much as numbers—build financial partnerships that last.

By adopting these strategies, you can position yourself for long-term financial success and resilience, ensuring you are well-prepared for the evolving landscape of business credit.

10

LEVERAGING CREDIT FOR COMPETITIVE ADVANTAGE

"Credit, when handled wisely, can transform the way you compete in the marketplace. It is not merely a financial resource but a strategic asset that, when nurtured, opens doors to opportunities that many overlook."

When business credit is managed with precision and purpose, it becomes much more than a line on your balance sheet. It becomes an instrument for growth, a way to do more than your competitors, and a gateway to international markets. In this chapter, the focus is on turning your established credit profile into a distinct advantage—a competitive edge that sets your business apart in a crowded marketplace.

This chapter provides detailed, practical strategies that help you harness credit in ways that improve your market position, drive customer acquisition, and support expansion beyond local borders. The insights shared here stem from real-life

Shameka Landers

experiences, financial best practices, and the kind of straightforward thinking that has guided many successful entrepreneurs. By the end of this chapter, you will have a wealth of ideas, actionable steps, and reflective exercises to help you use your credit profile as a lever for competitive growth.

THE ROLE OF CREDIT IN GAINING MARKET ADVANTAGE

Business credit is more than what you use to secure loans or manage cash flow—it is a symbol of trust and reliability. Suppliers, lenders, and partners see a strong credit history as a proof that your business is dependable and ready to take on new challenges. Because the business sector is competitive already, this reputation can be the difference between being overlooked and being chosen as a preferred partner.

Why Credit Matters for Competitive Advantage

Credit is a cornerstone of financial reputation. A good credit profile can help your business in many ways.

- A very strong credit history most times results in lower interest rates, higher credit limits, and more flexible payment schedules. These will help your business to invest in growth without compromising cash flow.

- Most vendors and suppliers are more likely to offer better terms, discounts, and priority services to businesses that can prove to them that they have financial discipline.

- When you are negotiating contracts—whether for supplies, services, or partnerships—a healthy credit profile will put you in a position that will lead to more favorable agreements.

- If you are one of the business owners that is finding a way to enter international markets, credit becomes your passport to global trade. It will help you in creating vendor accounts abroad and securing financing in diverse economic environments.

- A reputable credit record will give an idea of stability and reliability, enhancing your brand's image and building trust with customers and investors alike.

- The ability to quickly access funds allows you to react to market shifts and take advantage of time-sensitive opportunities.

Take a moment to consider the following questions:

- How has your current credit profile influenced your business relationships?

- In what ways have favorable credit terms allowed you to seize new opportunities?

- What challenges have you encountered when trying to secure financing or better terms from suppliers?

If you can provide a genuine answer to these questions, it will help you pinpoint areas where leveraging credit could further enhance your competitive advantage.

USING CREDIT TO OUTPACE COMPETITORS

One of the primary advantages of a strong credit profile is the ability to react quickly to market opportunities. When competitors are hampered by limited access to capital, your business—backed by reliable credit—can make bold moves.

A good credit foundation means you can seize any opportunity that requires fast decision-making and immediate investment. Consider these scenarios:

- When a surge in demand occurs, having a solid credit line will allow you to have inventory in bulk, most times at discounted rates, ensuring that you never miss a sale.

- Whether you have a plan to open a new branch or expand your current facilities, or even both, fast access to credit means you can move ahead without waiting for cash reserves to build.

- A strong credit profile allows you to launch aggressive marketing campaigns or rebrand quickly, capturing market share before competitors catch up.

- The avenue to offer competitive salaries and invest in training becomes easier when you have access to favorable credit terms, enabling you to build a stronger, more innovative team.

Detailed Examples

- **Inventory Opportunities:** Imagine a seasonal spike where competitors struggle to meet demand. With a flexible line of credit, you can purchase inventory at off-peak pricing and secure stock before prices rise.

- **Operational Expansion:** When a promising new market emerges, having immediate access to funds means you can open a new outlet or expand an existing one before competitors even start planning.

- **Brand Visibility:** In industries where first impressions matter, timely investments in a comprehensive marketing campaign can position your brand as the leader in innovation and reliability.

- **Technological Upgrades:** Investing in modern equipment or software not only increases efficiency but also signals to clients and partners that your business is forward-thinking and reliable.

Interactive Exercise

Write down a list of recent opportunities that you could have seized if better credit terms had been available. Next to each opportunity, note how improved credit could have changed the outcome. Use these notes to guide future borrowing strategies that align with your growth objectives.

LEVERAGING CREDIT FOR INTERNATIONAL EXPANSION

Expanding into international markets is something that is both exciting and challenging at the same time. While local markets may offer you stability, international expansion will open up a door of opportunities—multiple revenue streams, accessing new customer bases, and tapping into global supply chains. Credit is an essential tool for businesses venturing into new territories.

To compete on an international stage, it's a must that your credit profile speaks the language of global finance. This does not mean that you only maintain excellent domestic credit ratings but also understand how credit is perceived in different countries. A reputable credit history can ease the process of:

- **Creating an International Vendor Account:** Suppliers in foreign markets are more inclined to extend credit if they see a well-documented record of timely payments and financial stability.

- **Accessing International Financial Support:** Creditworthiness is determined by banks and other financial institutions around the world using both domestic and global standards. A solid domestic credit history might be used as a benchmark.

- **Understanding Foreign Regulations:** Strict financial rules are common in many nations. Strong credit profiles may help you to reduce financial risk worries and assist to streamline regulatory clearance processes.

- **Building Trust with Foreign Partners:** Business partners overseas are more willing to work with businesses that demonstrate financial discipline and stability through a strong credit record.

- **Facilitating Currency Management:** A strong credit record can improve your access to financial instruments that help manage currency fluctuations, protecting your profit margins.

STRATEGIES FOR BUILDING GLOBAL CREDIT

Here are several practical strategies to prepare for and leverage credit in international expansion:

- **Try to Create Local Business Entities:** You can consider creating new subsidiaries or local branches in target markets to build a separate but related credit profile.

- **Work with International Banks:** Try to build relationships with banks that you know that they have a global presence. These banks can offer help that is tailored to businesses like yours with international aspirations.

- **Diversify Credit Instruments:** To control risk, combine vendor accounts, foreign exchange hedging tools, and overseas lines of credit.

- **Use Local Consultants:** Bear it in mind that local financial advisors or consultants with expertise in the target market can guide you through regulatory requirements and credit-building practices.

- **Put Your Eyes on Global Economic Indicators:** Stay informed about the latest economic trends in the regions you plan to enter. This awareness will help you expect changes in credit terms and adjust your strategy accordingly.

- **Have Proper Financial Documentation:** Ensure that all financial records are accurate, up-to-date, and compliant with both domestic and international standards. Transparency builds trust across borders.

- **Engage in International Trade Associations:** Find your way around networking with your fellow industries and join trade groups that can provide insights into local credit practices and facilitate introductions to potential financial partners.

Reflective Questions for You

- What markets have you identified as potential areas for expansion, and how does your current credit profile align with the requirements of these markets?

- How might establishing a local credit presence in a foreign market help you secure better terms or build stronger vendor relationships?

- Consider the regulatory challenges in your target market. What steps can you take to ensure that your credit profile meets international standards?

ENHANCING CUSTOMER ACQUISITION THROUGH FINANCIAL STRENGTH

Competitive advantage is not only limited to operational or market expansion; it also plays a major role in how you attract and retain customers. A business that demonstrates financial strength and stability inspires confidence in its customers. Here are some ways in which leveraging credit can directly enhance your customer acquisition strategies.

Building a Trustworthy Brand Image

Customers will go for any business that exudes stability and reliability. A strong credit profile is a silent endorsement of your business's ability to meet its financial obligations, and it translates into several customer-facing benefits:

- **Improved Service Capabilities:** Having more money allows you to make investments in enhancing customer service, maximizing processes, and guaranteeing that the quality of your goods or services stays high.

- **Enhanced Marketing Efforts:** Better credit terms make it possible for bigger and better marketing efforts to build brand recognition and loyal customer bases.

- **Competitive Prices:** If you can get low-interest loans, you can lower your operating costs and offer competitive prices without lowering the quality of your products.
- **Better Customer Support:** Putting money into strong customer support systems makes customers feel appreciated and cared for, which boosts trust and word-of-mouth advertising.
- **More money to invest in new ideas:** If you're financially stable, you can keep improving and coming up with new ideas for your products and services, which keeps your business fresh and attractive.
- **Better operational efficiency:** Getting more money can help improve operations, which can speed up service delivery and make customers happier.
- **Better After-Sales Services:** You can improve your after-sales services by adding things like insurance, upkeep programs, and support hotlines. This will help customers feel good about the purchases they make.

Detailed Customer Acquisition Tactics

Consider these tactics to transform your financial advantage into tangible customer benefits:

- **Programs that reward or encourage repeat business:** Start programs that reward or encourage repeat business. Give your best customers special deals, early access to new goods, or events that no one else can attend.
- **Improvements to the customer experience:** Spend money to improve your online platforms, build up your

customer service teams, or fix up your old buildings. These changes bring in new customers and help keep old ones coming back.
- **Campaigns for advertising:** Create marketing efforts that use a variety of channels and stress the security and innovation of your brand. To build a good reputation, use social media, neighborhood ads, and community events.
- **Flexible Payment Options:** Give customers the chance to finance their purchases or set up payment plans over time. Customers may feel more safe making bigger purchases when they see that your business is stable financially.
- **Community Engagement:** Get involved with the people in your area by sponsoring events, giving money to charities, or doing other things. These kinds of actions build trust and improve the image of your brand.
- **After-Sales Support:** Make after-sales services better by adding things like longer warranties, free upkeep checks, or specialized support lines. Customer service that goes above and beyond can turn one-time buyers into lifelong supporters.
- **Feedback and Improvement:** To keep making your services better, get feedback from customers on a regular basis and look it over. Credit should be used wisely to make investments in areas where making changes will greatly increase customer happiness.

STRATEGIC CONSIDERATIONS AND RISK MANAGEMENT

Using credit for competitive advantage requires a careful balance between seizing opportunities and managing potential risks. While taking bold steps can lead to significant gains, it is essential to maintain a level of caution that protects your business from overextension and unforeseen setbacks.

Balancing Growth with Financial Prudence

As you push forward to outpace competitors, it is vital to manage risk effectively. Consider these strategies:

- **Keep Enough Cash at Hand:** You should always keep some of your cash available to pay off debt. This reserve is used as a safety net in case the market changes or goes down unexpectedly.
- **Spread out your investment channels:** Don't depend on just one source of funding. Trade lines, business credit cards, term loans, and foreign financing tools should all be used together.
- **Review financial metrics on a regular basis:** Set up key performance indicators (KPIs) to keep an eye on how credit is being used, cash flow, debt-to-income rates, and the general health of your finances. When you do regular reviews, you can make changes at the right time.
- **Make financial models for the best-case, worst-case, and most likely situations as part of scenario planning:** This practice helps you get ready for the unknown and makes sure you're ready to change direction when you need to.
- **Do Risk Assessments:** Look at the possible risks that come with new loan applications, business efforts in other countries, or large-scale marketing campaigns on a regular basis. Figure out what could go wrong with cash flow and make plans to fix the problems.
- **Get Professional Help:** If you're going into a market you don't know much about or a financing system that is hard to understand, talk to a financial advisor or a lawyer to help you make decisions.

- **Set up strict financial controls:** To make sure you don't spend too much, use budgeting tools, regular checks, and thorough financial reports. This mistake lowers the chance of taking on too much debt and bad management.
- **Keep an eye on global economic trends:** Keep up with foreign economic indicators that could have an effect on your markets, and change how you handle loans to lower the risks that could happen.
- **Prepare for the worst:** Get ready for quick drops in the economy by making clear plans for how to handle shortfalls in funds or sudden changes in the market.

Detailed Risk Management Checklist

Here are several key elements to include in your risk management plan:

- **Emergency Fund Adequacy:** Is your reserve sufficient to cover three to six months of operating expenses?

- **Debt Load Analysis:** Are current debt levels sustainable relative to your revenue and growth projections?

- **Credit Diversity:** Do you have a healthy mix of different credit types to reduce dependency on any single source?

- **Market Volatility Preparedness:** Have you modeled potential impacts of economic downturns or currency fluctuations on your international operations?

- **Vendor Relationship Health:** Are your relationships with suppliers and financial partners strong enough to secure renegotiated terms if needed?

- **Compliance and Regulation:** Is your business up-to-date with both domestic and international regulatory requirements to avoid legal pitfalls?

- **Communication Protocols:** Are there clear, documented processes for communicating financial challenges and updates across your management team?

- **Performance Review Frequency:** How often do you conduct financial reviews, and are the insights actionable?

- **Contingency Strategies:** What measures are in place if a key financing partner changes their terms unexpectedly?

CRAFTING YOUR PERSONAL CREDIT STRATEGY FOR COMPETITIVE GROWTH

Turning your credit profile into a competitive advantage requires careful planning, commitment, and a willingness to adapt to changing market conditions. Here are several steps to help you craft a personalized strategy:

Step 1: Assess Your Current Financial Standing

- **Take a look at your financial statements:** The income statements, balance sheets, and cash flow reports that you have should all be thoroughly examined.
- **Conduct a Credit Report Analysis:** First, you should get your most recent credit report from the main

agencies, and then you should search for areas where you can improve and regions where you can improve.
- **Carry out a SWOT Analysis:** In regard to your current financial situation and market position, it is important to identify the strengths, weaknesses, opportunities, and threats that your company will face.
- **Obtain the Services of Financial Advisors:** When looking for an outsider's point of view on your financial situation, you might want to think about talking with a reliable financial counselor or mentor.

Step 2: Set Clear and Measurable Goals

- **Define Short-Term Objectives:** Identify immediate improvements in credit terms or supplier relationships that could benefit your business within the next six to twelve months.
- **Outline Long-Term Aspirations:** Envision where you want your business to be in five or ten years, including market expansion, international operations, and diversification strategies.
- **Develop Action Plans:** For each goal, create a detailed action plan that includes specific steps, timelines, and responsible parties.

Step 3: Implement Strategic Financial Controls

- **Automate Financial Processes:** Utilize accounting software to automate invoicing, payment reminders, and cash flow tracking.
- **Establish Regular Financial Reviews:** Schedule monthly or quarterly meetings to review financial performance and discuss adjustments.

Shameka Landers

- **Create Detailed Budgets:** Develop comprehensive budgets that include projections for revenue, expenses, and debt repayments.
- **Monitor Key Performance Indicators (KPIs):** Track metrics such as credit utilization, debt-to-income ratios, and supplier payment terms.
- **Conduct Periodic Audits:** Regularly audit your financial records to ensure accuracy and transparency.

Step 4: Engage Continuously with Stakeholders

- **Maintain Open Communication:** Keep lines of communication open with suppliers, lenders, and financial partners to build trust and secure favorable terms.
- **Solicit Feedback:** Regularly ask for input from your management team and financial advisors to refine your strategy.
- **Document Lessons Learned:** Maintain a record of successes and challenges to inform future decision-making.

Step 5: Embrace Flexibility and Continuous Improvement

- **Stay Informed:** Keep up with industry trends by reading publications, attending conferences, and networking with other business owners.
- **Be Ready to Pivot:** If a strategy isn't working, be prepared to adjust and explore alternative approaches.
- **Celebrate Milestones:** Recognize and celebrate achievements to maintain motivation and momentum.

CONCLUSION

The credit profile of a company goes much beyond its borrowing capacity assessment. It is the evidence of your financial discipline, a warning to partners and clients, and a strategic tool that will help your company out ahead of the competition. Using a proactive, human-centered strategy to maximize credit will help you to:

- Confidently grab chances for development.
- Create enduring bonds with lenders, vendors, and consumers.
- Grow into both home and foreign new markets.

- Improve the standing of your brand as a consistent, creative market participant.
- Reduce risks even as you pursue audacious, strategic goals.
- Raise operational effectiveness and customer service standards.

Remember that every financial choice you make might change the course of your company as you consider the techniques, real-life case studies, and interactive activities this chapter presents. The competitive advantage is not only about credit availability; it is also about wise, innovative, and responsible use of that credit to create a company strong in any state of the economy.

Spend some time now looking over your present financial policies and thinking about how you may apply these ideas to your business.

Every choice adds value. Every prompt payment, smart investment, and cautious negotiation adds to a heritage of market leadership and financial stability. Let your credit be the

Shameka Landers

impetus for change; let it propel your company into unprecedented success.

11

RISK MANAGEMENT IN CREDIT USE

> *"Risk is inherent in every financial decision, but managing that risk with foresight and discipline transforms uncertainty into opportunity."*

In business credit, risk management is not about avoiding all obstacles; rather, it is about planning for them, reducing their influence, and building a strong framework that promotes sustainable development even in cases of unanticipated events. This chapter offers useful techniques and reflection activities meant to help you control credit problems. This chapter emphasizes on developing resilience, guaranteeing stability, and encouraging a proactive attitude to financial risk that will eventually protect your company.

UNDERSTANDING THE NATURE OF CREDIT RISK

Every financial choice has some risk. Risk management in the context of business credit involves knowing possible hazards and acting deliberately to avoid them. Among the several causes of credit risk are operational errors, market volatility, and outside economic pressure. Effective management of these major areas of credit risk starts with their recognition:

- Changes in market circumstances, interest rates, or economic downturns can influence loan ability to be repaid as well as borrowing cost.
- Effective processes, bad cash flow management, and unexpected spending can all strain your credit profile.
- Vendor and Lender connections: Unexpected financial strain results from changes in credit conditions or connections breaking down.
- Changing legal rules and international norms could affect credit agreements and incur extra expenses.
- Digital age fraud and cyber-attacks seriously jeopardize financial stability by means of their capacity to generate false actions.

By knowing these risks, you can create a clearer picture of your risk landscape, which will serve as a foundation for the strategies to come.

STRATEGIES FOR MITIGATING CREDIT RISK

Managing risk is about balancing opportunity with caution. The following strategies provide a framework to help you maintain control over your credit while still taking advantage of growth opportunities.

1. Establish a Comprehensive Risk Assessment Framework

Before making any significant financial decision, carry out a thorough risk assessment. This process should include:

- **Scenario Planning:** Model several scenarios—from best-case to worst-case—and find out how each might affect your debt, cash flow, and general financial situation. What happens, for example, if income suddenly declines by twenty percent? This would impair your capacity to pay debt.

- **SWOT Analysis:** In regard to credit utilization, list the strengths, weaknesses, opportunities, and threats of your company. Knowing your own shortcomings, including ineffective billing processes, will help you to improve these areas.

- **Frequent Review:** Plan weekly or quarterly analyses of your risk profile. These analyses have to examine changes in supplier terms, market trends, and interest rate modifications. Being proactive allows one to identify early warning signals and implement corrections.

2. Diversify Your Credit Sources

Relying on just one type of credit or a single lender can increase risk significantly. A varied credit portfolio offers a safeguard:

- Use many kinds of vendor accounts, business credit cards, revolving lines of credit, and term loans in a blend of credit tools. Each one has a different purpose and offers a different degree of adaptability.

- Work with several financial partners rather than depending only on one. This increases your options and encourages a competitive environment that can lead to better lending conditions.

Shameka Landers

- Other finance: Think about non-traditional choices, including invoice finance or revenue-based financing. In times of market downturn, these choices might provide additional degrees of safety.

- International Credit Lines: To lessen the effect of local economic fluctuations, people involved in worldwide markets might find it helpful to apply credit from foreign banks or financial organizations.

3. Maintain Adequate Cash Reserves

Cash reserves serve as your protective pillow during challenging periods. Here are several methods to establish and uphold them:

- **Emergency Money:** Set aside cash that are sufficient for at least three to six months' worth of operational expenditures. This is the emergency reserve. It is important that this reserve be liquid and quickly accessible in order to offset any unanticipated deficiencies.
- **Automated Savings:** Put in place procedures that will automatically set aside a certain proportion of your organization's revenue for your reserve fund. It is essential to be consistent; even little sums saved on a daily basis may build up to a large amount over time.
- **Expense Management:** In order to improve your cash flow, you should routinely analyze and reduce costs that are not required. Having an effective strategy for controlling costs guarantees that there will be more cash available for savings.
- **Contingency Planning:** Create comprehensive preparations for how your company will continue to function in the event of an interruption in the financial system. Among these options are the acquisition of

temporary credit lines and the postponement of expenses that are not essential.

4. Strengthen Operational Processes

Strong internal systems can reduce running risks and guarantee that you are ready to handle credit properly through the following ways:

- **Monitor Your Cash Flow:** Watch your cash flow closely and use forecasting techniques to project future shortages or surpluses. This facilitates debt payback planning and knowledge of when further credit could be required.
- **Apply rigorous financial control:** Create checks and balances for every credit-related purchase. Clear approval procedures, frequent audits, and duty separation help to lower fraud or mistake risk.
- **Make technology investments:** Track every transaction with consistent accounting tools and connected financial management systems. Real-time data can point to abnormalities before they cause major problems.
- **Prepare Your Team:** Frequent financial management and credit policy training courses guarantee that all participants value risk reduction and follow top standards.

5. Monitor External Factors

Managing risk depends on keeping current with outside events:

- **In terms of markets:** Track closely industry developments, rival actions, and economic data. Knowing changes in the market lets you modify your credit plan early on.
- **Regulatory Updates:** Keep informed on local and global developments in financial rules. Maintaining your credit reputation calls for compliance; it is not optional.
- **Lender Communications and Vendor Notes:** Talk often with your financial partners to keep updated on any possible credit term or lending policy changes.
- **Global Economic Indicators:** If your company deals overseas, keep an eye on trade rules, political changes that can affect your credit situation, and currency swings.

6. Use Insurance and Hedging Instruments

Financial hedging and insurance can offer even another level of defense through:

- **Credit Insurance:** Think about getting credit insurance to defend against important account non-payment or default. This controls any losses and safeguards cash flow.
- **Hedging Strategies:** Hedge against negative currency movements or interest rate swings via forward contracts, options, or swaps.
- **Agreements for Risk-Sharing:** Look at performance-based contracts that match risk with results, where your company shares it with lenders or suppliers.
- **Liability Insurance:** From operational mistakes to outside conflicts, be sure your liability insurance covers unanticipated occurrences influencing your business credit.

BUILDING A CULTURE OF PROACTIVE RISK MANAGEMENT

One person or department cannot handle risk; it is something that your whole company should have ingrained in its culture. The methods below guarantee that every team member recognizes the value of credit risk and coordinates to properly control it.

Fostering Financial Literacy

Teach your staff the fundamentals of credit risk, how it impacts the company, and the part each individual contributes to reducing that risk. This might include:

- Frequent financial management training courses or seminars.
- Presenting case stories of both achievements and difficulties together with best practices.
- Promoting a conversation whereby team members could provide fresh approaches for risk control.

Encouraging Accountability

Set up systems that encourage responsibility by:

- Clearly assigning people for handling financial data.
- Reward staff members who spot and use risk- or cost-cutting strategies.
- Make sure there are open channels of contact so that one may report such problems without thinking about consequences.

Celebrating Successes

When risk management strategies yield positive results, celebrate those wins:

- Acknowledge team members who contributed to successful cost-cutting or risk mitigation.
- Share stories of how proactive risk management helped avoid major pitfalls.
- Use these successes as case studies to refine and improve your risk management framework.

Remember that risk management in credit use is an ongoing journey, not a one-time task. Every decision, every process, and every strategy must be continually evaluated against changing circumstances and new challenges. By integrating proactive risk management into your daily operations, you create a business environment that is both dynamic and resilient—one where opportunities can be pursued confidently, even in the face of uncertainty.

As you move forward, remember:

- **Risk can be a catalyst for growth** if managed well.

- **Every proactive measure**—from diversifying credit sources to maintaining robust operational controls—builds a stronger foundation.

- **Engage your team,** gather feedback, and make continuous improvements to stay ahead.

- **Prepare for the unexpected** by maintaining adequate cash reserves and conducting regular scenario planning.

Shameka Landers

12

USING BUSINESS CREDIT TO IMPROVE OPERATIONS

"A well-oiled operation is the heartbeat of a successful business. When credit is used to streamline processes and boost efficiency, every dollar works harder for you."

Operational efficiency is not just a need in the dynamic market of today; it also surpasses mere competitive advantage. When handled sensibly, business credit may be a spark to turn daily operations into a powerhouse of output. This chapter provides doable tactics to help you maximize your credit to modernize systems, make technological investments, and build a lean supply chain. The aim is to provide you with practical insights to maximize your operations, lower expenses, and eventually raise your bottom line.

THE INTERSECTION OF CREDIT AND OPERATIONAL EFFICIENCY

For many businesses, keeping operations running smoothly can feel like an uphill battle, especially when cash flow is tight and resources are stretched. The ability to finance improvements often determines whether a business merely survives or thrives. Business credit plays a pivotal role in bridging these gaps, offering companies the flexibility to invest in vital improvements that might otherwise be unattainable. More than just a tool for borrowing, credit becomes a strategic resource for reinvesting in operational excellence, paving the way for growth, innovation, and long-term sustainability.

A well-managed credit strategy enables businesses to strengthen their operations in multiple ways:

- **Investing in Technology:** Businesses today thrive on automation and efficiency. Credit allows companies to invest in technology that streamlines operations, enhances data accuracy, and improves decision-making, ensuring they remain competitive.

- **Streamlining Processes:** From inventory management to customer service, adopting digital tools that integrate operations reduces inefficiencies, saves time, and enhances productivity.

- **Enhancing Supply Chain Efficiency:** Credit gives businesses the leverage to negotiate better terms with suppliers, purchase materials in bulk at discounted rates, and optimize logistics to avoid costly delays or disruptions.

- **Improving Workforce Productivity:** Employees are the backbone of any operation. Using credit to fund training programs, provide modern tools, and upgrade workspaces fosters a more efficient and motivated workforce.

- **Expanding Operational Capabilities:** As businesses scale, their operational demands increase. Credit can support expansion efforts by covering costs for facility upgrades, additional equipment, or increased production capacity—without exhausting cash reserves.

INVESTING IN TECHNOLOGY AND AUTOMATION

Using technology and automation is one of the most important approaches to enhance processes. Credit can give the financial backing required to use cutting-edge technologies aiming at efficiency and minimal human mistakes in the following ways:

- Install systems that automatically handle mundane chores such as order processing, inventory control, and billing.
- Move to cloud-based solutions in project management, customer relationship management (CRM), and accounting.
- Invest in analytics to monitor important performance indicators (KPIs) and obtain an understanding of operational efficiency.
- Allocate money for strong cybersecurity software to guard private information and uphold consumer confidence.

  Give your staff mobile tools and apps that let them remotely access running systems.
- Use software that combines several capabilities—including sales, inventory, and customer service—into one smooth platform.

Detailed Examples

- **Automated Inventory Management:** Automatically reorders stock as levels dip below a set threshold.

- **Real-Time Financial Reporting:** Cloud-based accounting software enables real-time tracking of expenses and cash flow.

- **Enhanced Customer Relationship Management:** CRM systems track customer interactions, leading to better service and retention.

STRATEGIES TO OPTIMIZE PROCESSES WITH CREDIT

Efficient processes are the backbone of any successful operation. When you leverage credit to streamline your operations, you create a more agile, responsive business capable of meeting customer needs quickly and effectively.

- **Process Mapping:** Identify bottlenecks, redundancies, and areas where delays occur.

- **Investing in Process Improvement Initiatives:** Fund projects such as Lean Six Sigma training, process reengineering, or technology upgrades.

- **Outsourcing Non-Core Functions:** Use credit to delegate tasks like IT support or payroll processing to external experts.

- **Employee Training and Development:** Allocate credit toward comprehensive training programs that empower employees.

- **Implementing Feedback Systems:** Develop internal systems to gather employee feedback on process improvements.

- **Regular Process Audits:** Schedule audits to identify opportunities for further optimization.

ENHANCING SUPPLY CHAIN EFFICIENCY

A well-managed supply chain is essential for operational success. Business credit can be instrumental in optimizing your supply chain by providing the financial flexibility to negotiate better terms, invest in logistics, and build stronger relationships with suppliers.

Key Areas to Focus On

- Bulk Purchasing and Inventory Management
- Technology in Supply Chain Management
- Vendor Relationship Management
- Logistics and Distribution
- Risk Mitigation

Detailed Examples

- **Inventory Financing:** Use business credit to finance inventory purchases during peak seasons.

- **Integrated Supply Chain Software:** Implement software that integrates with your ordering systems for real-time updates.

Shameka Landers

- **Vendor Consolidation:** Negotiate long-term contracts with key suppliers by leveraging your strong credit profile.

CONCLUSION

Using business credit to improve operations is an ongoing journey that transforms the way your business functions from the inside out. By investing in technology, streamlining processes, optimizing your supply chain, and exploring new markets, you create a robust, agile operation that stands ready to meet the challenges of a dynamic business environment.

As you reflect on the strategies outlined in this chapter, remember:

- Operational efficiency is the foundation upon which sustainable growth is built.

- Leveraging business credit is not about borrowing more—it's about borrowing smartly.

- A culture of continuous improvement ensures that your business stays ahead of market trends and operational challenges.

Take some time to review your current operational processes. Identify the areas where business credit could make the biggest impact, and develop an action plan to implement the changes. With a strategic approach and a commitment to excellence, you can transform your operations into a model of efficiency and innovation—setting the stage for future growth and success.

13

HOW SUCCESSFUL ENTREPRENEURS USE BUSINESS CREDIT

"Credit is more than a financial tool; it is a catalyst for strategic growth when used wisely."

Successful entrepreneurs understand that business credit is not just a means of acquiring funds—it is a tool that, when leveraged properly, drives growth, strengthens financial resilience, and expands opportunities. The businesses that thrive are those that see credit as a strategic asset rather than a liability. By analyzing the habits of successful entrepreneurs, we can uncover key practices that transform business credit into a cornerstone of sustainable success.

LEVERAGING BUSINESS CREDIT FOR EXPANSION AND SCALABILITY

Entrepreneurs who scale their businesses effectively recognize that growth often requires more capital than what is available in cash reserves. Business credit enables them to expand operations, enter new markets, and enhance their product or service offerings without jeopardizing their liquidity. The ability to strategically leverage credit allows businesses to grow at a pace that matches market demands rather than being constrained by available cash flow.

Expanding Operations Without Straining Cash Flow

Rather than waiting to accumulate cash reserves, many business owners use credit to finance expansion efforts such as opening new locations, upgrading facilities, or hiring additional staff. By securing credit lines with favorable terms, they ensure their business can scale while maintaining financial stability. The key is to plan expansion carefully, taking into account repayment terms, projected revenue growth, and return on investment.

A well-planned expansion involves a combination of long-term and short-term financing strategies. Entrepreneurs often utilize revolving credit lines for operational expenses while securing term loans for major capital expenditures. This approach ensures that businesses maintain liquidity while still taking advantage of growth opportunities.

Case Study: Expanding a Retail Chain

A small retail entrepreneur built a loyal customer base in a single location. Recognizing the potential to replicate success in a neighboring city, they leveraged a business line of credit to secure a second retail space, purchase inventory, and launch a localized marketing campaign. To mitigate financial risk, they also established vendor credit arrangements, reducing the need for upfront capital on inventory purchases. Additionally, they used their existing strong credit history to negotiate favorable lease terms, lowering initial overhead costs.

Within a year, the new location became profitable, reinforcing the entrepreneur's confidence in using credit strategically for expansion. They continued this approach, opening multiple locations in new markets, each expansion carefully structured to maximize the benefits of business credit while minimizing financial strain.

STRENGTHENING SUPPLIER RELATIONSHIPS THROUGH SMART CREDIT MANAGEMENT

Successful business owners know that strong supplier relationships are the foundation of smooth business operations. A well-structured and managed credit profile not only fosters credibility but also provides an opportunity to secure favorable terms that enhance operational efficiency and cost management. Entrepreneurs who understand the importance of supplier relationships leverage business credit to create long-term partnerships that yield financial benefits.

Negotiating Better Terms with Vendors

A strong credit history gives businesses negotiating power, enabling them to secure extended payment terms, discounted bulk pricing, and exclusive supplier incentives. By consistently demonstrating financial responsibility, business owners gain the confidence of their vendors, who may be more inclined to offer flexible arrangements. Such agreements improve cash flow, allowing businesses to reinvest in other areas such as marketing, product development, or expansion.

Beyond payment terms, suppliers often prioritize financially stable businesses when distributing limited inventory during peak seasons. A business with a reliable credit record is more likely to receive priority stock allocations, avoiding supply chain disruptions that could impact sales and customer satisfaction.

Example: Building Trust with Key Suppliers

A restaurant owner, after diligently managing their credit and maintaining an impeccable payment record, was able to negotiate net-60 terms with their primary food suppliers. This agreement allowed the restaurant to order ingredients without immediate upfront payments, providing a 60-day buffer to generate revenue before settling invoices. As a result, the owner could maintain a more consistent inventory, reducing waste and ensuring fresh ingredients were always available. Furthermore, their supplier, recognizing the restaurant's reliability, offered additional bulk discounts, reducing overall costs. This strategic credit management approach gave the restaurant a competitive advantage over other establishments still operating on net-30 or immediate payment terms, ultimately improving profitability and sustainability.

USING CREDIT TO FUND INNOVATION AND COMPETITIVE DIFFERENTIATION

Innovation is a driving force behind the most successful businesses. Many industry leaders have utilized business credit to fund research and development (R&D), adopt new technologies, and improve customer experiences. Businesses that consistently innovate maintain a competitive edge by staying relevant in changing markets.

Investing in Research and Development

Many entrepreneurs understand that staying ahead requires continuous innovation. Business credit enables them to test new ideas, develop prototypes, and bring innovative products or services to market without depleting working capital. By leveraging credit to fund R&D, businesses can explore new solutions, enhance their offerings, and gain a technological advantage over competitors.

Business credit also plays a role in developing sustainable and eco-friendly practices. Companies investing in green technology often require substantial capital, and financing such initiatives through credit allows them to implement long-term environmental strategies without draining cash reserves.

Additionally, businesses that incorporate new technologies into their operations—such as artificial intelligence, automation, and big data analytics—position themselves for increased efficiency and profitability. Those who fail to invest in these areas often find themselves struggling to compete in a rapidly evolving marketplace.

Example: Tech Startup Funding Innovation

A software startup utilized a business credit card with cash-back rewards to fund early development costs. By using the rewards strategically to offset expenses, the company minimized its financial burden while perfecting its software. Additionally, they secured a credit line specifically for research, which enabled them to hire top-tier developers and conduct beta testing before launch. Eventually, the business attracted investor interest and scaled into a multi-million-dollar enterprise, proving that credit-fueled innovation can lead to sustainable growth and industry disruption.

In another example, a manufacturing company leveraged a business credit line to develop an eco-friendly packaging solution. Their investment in sustainable materials and production processes positioned them as an industry leader in environmentally responsible manufacturing. This innovation not only expanded their customer base but also opened doors to partnerships with large retailers that prioritized sustainability.

CONCLUSION

The most successful entrepreneurs don't just use credit—they master it. They understand that business credit is not merely about borrowing money but about creating financial leverage that fuels sustainable growth. By using credit strategically, they expand their operations, strengthen supplier relationships, invest in innovation, manage cash flow effectively, and maintain strong credit profiles.

For business owners looking to achieve long-term success, the key takeaway is clear: credit, when managed with foresight and discipline, is one of the most powerful tools in an entrepreneur's arsenal. Harnessing it wisely can mean the difference between stagnation and strategic expansion, between financial struggle and financial stability. By adopting the best practices of successful entrepreneurs, any business can build a strong financial foundation and thrive in an increasingly competitive landscape.

14

SMART LEADERSHIP AND TEAM MANAGEMENT

"Strong leadership isn't just about vision; it's about equipping your team with the tools and mindset to navigate challenges and seize opportunities."

Success in business isn't solely dependent on great ideas or strong financial backing—it is influenced mainly by effective leadership and team management. A business leader who understands the importance of credit, financial literacy, and strategic delegation creates an empowered workforce that thrives in a competitive market. This chapter is mainly about the traits of financially savvy leaders and the importance of financial education.

TRAITS OF FINANCIALLY SAVVY LEADERS

Great leaders do more than inspire; they make data-driven decisions, manage financial risks proactively, and cultivate an environment where employees understand the value of sound financial practices. Financially savvy leaders:

Shameka Landers

- **Prioritize Strategic Planning:** They assess business finances regularly, anticipate market fluctuations, and prepare contingency plans. They take a proactive approach to risk management, ensuring that their businesses remain resilient in the face of economic uncertainties. They don't just react to market changes; they prepare for them by analyzing trends, setting realistic financial goals, and maintaining a clear roadmap for future growth.

- **Make Informed Credit Decisions:** They leverage business credit to expand operations, improve cash flow, and finance strategic initiatives without overleveraging debt. They understand the importance of balancing short-term credit needs with long-term financial sustainability, ensuring that borrowed funds are used for investments that yield measurable returns rather than unnecessary expenses.

- **Emphasize Financial Transparency:** They maintain open communication about financial goals, ensuring their team understands the company's fiscal health and objectives. They cultivate a culture of trust by regularly sharing financial reports, budgets, and forecasts, allowing employees to align their efforts with the company's overall financial strategy.

- **Encourage Smart Budgeting:** They instill responsible financial habits within their organization, setting clear budgets and ensuring funds are allocated effectively. They encourage department heads to make informed spending decisions, track expenses diligently, and optimize resources to maximize efficiency and profitability.

Shameka Landers

- **Build a Culture of Accountability:** They empower team members by delegating financial responsibilities and fostering an ownership mindset. Employees are encouraged to treat company finances with the same level of care and responsibility as their personal finances, ensuring thoughtful decision-making and cost-consciousness at all levels of the organization.

- **Adapt and Innovate Financial Strategies:** They are not afraid to rethink financial practices and adapt to emerging financial trends. Whether it's leveraging new financial technologies, optimizing supply chain costs, or restructuring debt for better terms, they remain agile in their financial planning.

- **Develop Strong Relationships with Lenders and Investors:** They understand that access to capital is key for long-term business growth. By maintaining good credit and strong financial credibility, they position their businesses for favorable loan terms, investment opportunities, and financial partnerships that support expansion and innovation.

Consider the case of a mid-sized manufacturing firm that struggled with cash flow issues due to poor financial management. Suppliers were demanding immediate payments, and the company was often unable to purchase raw materials in bulk, leading to higher costs and inconsistent production cycles. The newly appointed CEO, recognizing the importance of financial literacy, mandated leadership training on credit management, cash flow forecasting, and supplier negotiations.

In addition to improving financial awareness, the CEO introduced structured financial policies that included optimizing vendor payment schedules, setting clear credit utilization limits, and enforcing disciplined budgeting practices across all departments. These initiatives not only stabilized cash flow but also enabled the company to secure better supplier terms, including extended payment periods and bulk discounts.

Within two years, the company optimized its credit utilization, reduced reliance on high-interest short-term loans, and improved supplier relationships, which led to a 30% increase in profit margins. By aligning leadership with financial discipline and ensuring that every department understood the importance of prudent financial management, the company turned its struggles into long-term success and positioned itself for sustainable growth.

BUILDING FINANCIAL LITERACY WITHIN LEADERSHIP TEAMS

A business is only as strong as its leadership team. Financial literacy among executives and managers ensures the organization remains resilient and adaptable. Financially literate leaders:

- Understand balance sheets, cash flow statements, and credit reports.

- Know how to access and utilize business credit wisely.

- Can evaluate financial risks and opportunities efficiently.

- Develop strategies to optimize funding sources and expenses.

- Are able to identify potential financial red flags before they become major issues.

- Possess negotiation skills to secure better deals from lenders, suppliers, and financial institutions.

- Can guide their teams in making financially responsible decisions that align with long-term business goals.

- Recognize opportunities for investment and know when to use credit to seize growth potential while mitigating financial risks.

To strengthen financial literacy within leadership teams, you can implement:

Financial Training Programs

Regular workshops on budgeting, credit management, and risk assessment equip leaders with essential skills. These training sessions help executives and managers make more confident financial decisions, ensuring the company's financial health remains a top priority. Ongoing education ensures leaders stay current with market trends, new financial tools, and evolving business practices.

Data-Driven Decision-Making Tools

Providing managers with financial dashboards and analytics tools enables them to make informed choices. Access to real-time data ensures that leadership teams can monitor business performance, identify inefficiencies, and optimize spending. These tools also help leaders set and adjust financial goals based on accurate forecasting models.

Cross-Departmental Financial Transparency

Encouraging collaboration between finance teams and department heads ensures everyone understands how financial decisions impact business objectives. This transparency fosters a unified approach to achieving financial stability and growth. When all leaders are aligned in financial strategy, budgeting becomes more efficient, and costly financial mistakes are avoided.

A financially literate leadership team acts as a safeguard against financial mismanagement, ensuring the business remains profitable, adaptable, and well-prepared for future challenges. By implementing these practices, businesses cultivate leaders who can drive financial success and sustain long-term growth.

15

TRANSITIONING FROM CREDIT RELIANCE TO FINANCIAL INDEPENDENCE

"Knowing when to shift from borrowing to self-sufficiency is the mark of a financially mature business."

Building a successful business often requires leveraging credit to fuel growth, maintain cash flow, and invest in expansion. However, as a business matures, reliance on credit should gradually decrease, paving the way for self-sustainability and financial independence. Smart entrepreneurs recognize that while credit is a powerful tool, long-term financial health depends on strategic reinvestment, disciplined spending, and maintaining a robust financial buffer.

THE SIGNS YOUR BUSINESS IS READY TO RELY LESS ON CREDIT

Not all businesses reach financial independence at the same pace. However, certain indicators signal when it may be time

Shameka Landers

to reduce dependency on credit and transition to more self-sustaining financial practices. These include:

- **Consistent Profitability:** Your business generates stable revenue and maintains profit margins without frequent reliance on credit for operating expenses.

- **Strong Cash Flow Management:** Cash flow remains positive, allowing your business to cover day-to-day costs, payroll, and emergency expenses without needing credit.

- **Low Debt-to-Income Ratio:** Your debt load is manageable, with a declining dependency on credit for operational needs.

- **Sufficient Emergency Funds:** You have built up a financial reserve that covers at least six months of operating expenses.

- **Established Business Creditworthiness:** Your credit profile is strong enough to allow access to favorable loan terms but is not needed for survival.

- **Investment in Growth Without Excessive Borrowing:** Expansion efforts are funded more by retained earnings than by new debt obligations.

Recognizing these signs ensures you shift toward financial independence in a sustainable manner, rather than prematurely cutting off access to necessary funding.

Shameka Landers

STRATEGIES FOR REDUCING CREDIT DEPENDENCE

Transitioning away from credit reliance requires strategic financial planning and disciplined execution. Below are key approaches to strengthening financial self-sufficiency:

1. Strengthening Cash Flow Management

Maintaining a healthy cash flow is the foundation of financial independence. This includes:

- **Accelerating Receivables:** Implement strategies such as early payment discounts for customers and enforcing timely invoice collection.

- **Delaying Payables Without Penalty:** While paying suppliers on time is essential, negotiating extended terms can keep more cash available for operations.

- **Monitoring Cash Flow Projections:** Keeping a detailed cash flow forecast ensures better financial planning and prevents unexpected shortfalls.

2. Reinvesting Profits Wisely

Instead of relying on credit to fund growth, reinvesting profits into the business allows for organic expansion. Ways to reinvest wisely include:

- **Upgrading Technology:** Automation and efficiency-improving tools reduce long-term costs and enhance productivity.

- **Employee Training and Development:** A well-trained workforce drives higher efficiency and better decision-making, reducing operational waste.

- **Marketing and Customer Retention Strategies:** Investing in sustainable customer acquisition and retention efforts leads to steady revenue growth without the need for borrowed capital.

3. Establishing a Business Savings Plan

Creating a robust financial reserve ensures that future expenses can be handled without resorting to credit. Steps to achieving this include:

- **Setting Aside a Percentage of Profits:** Allocate a portion of monthly earnings to an emergency or reinvestment fund.

- **Diversifying Savings Vehicles:** Consider high-yield savings accounts or business investment accounts for longer-term financial stability.

- **Avoiding Unnecessary Expenses:** Review budgets regularly to eliminate wasteful spending and increase savings potential.

4. Paying Down Debt Strategically

Reducing outstanding liabilities minimizes financial risk and improves business stability. Strategies to manage debt efficiently include:

- **Prioritizing High-Interest Debt:** Paying off high-cost debt first reduces long-term interest expenses.

Shameka Landers

- **Consolidating Loans Where Possible:** Refinancing into lower-interest options or consolidating multiple debts can simplify payments and reduce costs.

- **Making Extra Payments When Feasible:** Allocating surplus revenue toward early debt repayment accelerates financial independence.

LEVERAGING CREDIT FOR GROWTH WITHOUT DEPENDENCY

Eliminating unnecessary credit reliance does not mean abandoning credit entirely. Smart businesses use credit selectively, ensuring it serves as an enabler rather than a crutch.

When to Use Credit Strategically

- **For Expansion, Not Operations:** Using credit for new revenue-generating initiatives rather than for covering operational shortfalls.

- **For Bulk Purchases with Negotiable Terms:** Taking advantage of supplier discounts that improve profit margins.

- **For Building Credit History and Business Reputation:** Maintaining active but controlled credit use keeps credit scores strong and ensures access to funding when genuinely needed.

A growing e-commerce business initially relied on business credit cards and loans to manage inventory purchases, digital marketing expenses, and logistics costs. In the early stages, maintaining sufficient working capital was challenging, requiring frequent use of credit to cover fluctuations in cash flow. However, as the business scaled, they prioritized financial discipline by analyzing cash flow trends, reducing unnecessary expenses, and increasing profit margins through better pricing strategies.

Over time, they developed a structured financial management plan, which included optimizing inventory turnover rates, negotiating extended payment terms with suppliers, and implementing cost-effective marketing strategies. By reinvesting a percentage of their monthly profits into an emergency reserve, they built a financial cushion that enabled them to gradually reduce their reliance on credit.

Within five years, they successfully phased out short-term borrowing by leveraging retained earnings for operational expenses. The company also strengthened supplier relationships, securing bulk discounts and flexible payment terms, which further minimized their need for external financing. By the seventh year, credit was only used strategically for high-impact initiatives such as expanding product lines, opening new distribution channels, and testing new market segments, ensuring that borrowed capital directly contributed to long-term profitability rather than day-to-day operations.

THE LONG-TERM BENEFITS OF FINANCIAL INDEPENDENCE

Reducing credit reliance results in a stronger, more resilient business. The key advantages include:

- **Greater Financial Flexibility:** With less debt, more capital is available for strategic opportunities.

- **Improved Profitability:** Eliminating interest payments frees up revenue for reinvestment and growth.

- **Reduced Financial Stress:** A debt-free business can navigate economic downturns with confidence.

- **Enhanced Business Valuation:** Investors and potential buyers favor businesses with strong financials and minimal debt obligations.

Achieving financial independence is not about eliminating credit altogether but about using it intelligently. By shifting focus toward strategic reinvestment, disciplined cash flow management, and sustainable financial practices, businesses can secure long-term stability and success.

16

THE LEGACY OF SMART CREDIT USE

"The way a business manages credit today determines its financial legacy tomorrow."

Long-term success in business isn't just about making money—it's about sustaining financial health across generations. Smart credit use allows businesses to build a strong financial foundation, create lasting opportunities, and leave behind a legacy that fosters resilience, stability, and continued growth.

This final chapter explores how businesses can implement sustainable credit practices, create long-term financial strategies, and ensure that future leaders understand the importance of responsible financial management.

THE ROLE OF CREDIT IN BUILDING A LASTING BUSINESS LEGACY

A business that effectively manages its credit sets the stage for long-term prosperity. Whether a company is family-owned, a startup evolving into an industry leader, or a large corporation aiming for multi-generational sustainability, responsible credit use plays a crucial role in shaping its financial legacy.

A strong credit profile allows businesses to:

- **Secure Long-Term Financial Partnerships:** Strong creditworthiness ensures favorable terms with banks, investors, and lenders.

- **Enable Business Continuity:** A solid financial foundation supports smooth transitions during leadership changes and economic downturns.

- **Expand Without Overleveraging:** Strategic credit use supports controlled growth while minimizing financial risks.

- **Enhance Market Reputation:** Creditworthiness builds trust with stakeholders, including suppliers, employees, and customers.

Successful businesses maintain a balance between leveraging credit for growth and ensuring financial resilience through careful planning and disciplined credit management.

STRATEGIES FOR SUSTAINABLE CREDIT USE

Smart entrepreneurs don't just use credit when needed; they integrate it into their financial strategy to maintain stability and scalability. Here's how businesses can establish sustainable credit practices:

1. Maintaining a Healthy Credit Profile

A business's credit profile is like its financial report card. Consistently managing debt, making timely payments, and keeping a low credit utilization ratio contribute to a strong credit standing. Key practices include:

- **Monitoring Credit Reports Regularly:** Regularly reviewing business credit reports ensures accuracy and provides early warnings for potential financial risks.

- **Keeping Debt Levels Manageable:** Avoiding excessive debt helps businesses maintain flexibility and financial security.

- **Building Relationships with Lenders:** Long-term relationships with financial institutions can lead to better credit terms and access to exclusive funding opportunities.

2. Planning for Financial Stability

Even the most creditworthy businesses can face financial uncertainty. Preparing for downturns is essential to maintaining financial health. Strategies include:

- **Creating an Emergency Reserve:** Setting aside funds ensures credit isn't the only safety net during unexpected financial hardships.

- **Implementing Financial Forecasting:** Predicting cash flow fluctuations helps businesses plan ahead and avoid unnecessary borrowing.

- **Diversifying Revenue Streams:** Expanding business offerings or markets minimizes risk and ensures steady income.

For a business to leave a legacy, financial wisdom must be passed down to future generations of leaders. Training the next wave of business owners and executives in responsible credit management ensures continued financial success. Steps to achieve this include:

- **Developing Financial Education Programs:** Internal training sessions or mentoring programs help future leaders understand credit management and financial planning.

- **Documenting Credit Policies and Best Practices:** A well-documented approach to credit ensures continuity, even during leadership transitions.

- **Encouraging Financial Accountability:** Leaders should instill a culture of financial discipline and responsibility at all levels of the organization.

Case Study: A Multi-Generational Business

A family-owned manufacturing company successfully transitioned leadership across three generations by implementing structured financial policies. The company trained each generation in financial management, ensuring a deep understanding of responsible credit use. This approach allowed them to expand while maintaining financial health, leaving a lasting legacy of success and stability.

THE IMPACT OF RESPONSIBLE CREDIT USE ON BUSINESS REPUTATION

A company's credit management affects how it is perceived in the market. Businesses with strong credit histories gain credibility with lenders, suppliers, and investors. Positive financial reputation leads to:

- **Stronger Business Partnerships:** Suppliers and lenders are more likely to offer favorable terms.

- **Increased Investment Opportunities:** A well-managed credit profile attracts potential investors.

- **Higher Business Valuation:** Buyers and stakeholders assess financial history when considering mergers or acquisitions.

Leaving behind a strong financial legacy means ensuring future business leaders are equipped with the right financial tools and knowledge. Smart credit management should be a core principle in every business, regardless of industry or size. By focusing on sustainable credit use, financial education, and responsible decision-making, businesses can create a lasting impact that benefits future generations.

A business's legacy is not just measured by its success today but by its ability to thrive in the future. By integrating disciplined credit management, strategic financial planning, and a commitment to financial education, companies can set the stage for sustained growth and long-term stability.

Shameka Landers

CONCLUSION

The journey through these pages has been a deep one into the diverse world of business credit—a journey that has taken you from the very foundations of understanding credit to mastering its advanced, strategic uses. At every turn, the goal has been to empower you with the knowledge, tools, and confidence needed to build a resilient financial future for your business.

Over the course of this guide, you learned that business credit is much more than a number or a means to secure funding. It is the very bedrock upon which scalable, sustainable growth is built. Whether you are just beginning to formalize your business or are well on your way to leveraging credit for competitive advantage, the principles outlined here serve as a roadmap for financial success.

Yet, the journey doesn't end with theory. As a final reminder of the fundamentals, consider these **first 12 steps** when applying for credit—a quick reference that encapsulates many of the critical points you've encountered in this book:

1. **LLCs or Corporations** – Forming a formal business entity is essential for building and protecting your business credit.

2. **Commercial Address** – Having a dedicated business location (even if virtual) signals legitimacy to lenders.

3. **EIN Number** – This is your business's equivalent of a Social Security Number, critical for separating personal and company finances.

Shameka Landers

4. **Business License** – Demonstrates that your enterprise is properly registered and operating under the correct regulations.

5. **Business Bank Account** – Keeping personal and business finances separate is key to clear record-keeping and credible financials.

6. **SIC/NAICS Codes** – Ensuring your business is classified correctly can impact how lenders perceive risk in your industry.

7. **411 Listings** – Listing your business phone number publicly can bolster your professional image and creditworthiness.

8. **Business Email Address** – A dedicated email domain underscores professionalism and consistency in your brand.

9. **Website** – In today's digital world, a credible web presence signals stability and trustworthiness to both customers and creditors.

10. **Company Logo, Business Letterhead** – Unified branding reinforces the legitimacy and seriousness of your enterprise.

11. **Professional Voicemail** – A well-crafted, business-oriented voicemail greets lenders and partners with the professionalism they expect.

12. **Get a DUNS NUMBER** – A unique identifier from Dun & Bradstreet is pivotal for building your credit profile and unlocking new financial opportunities.

These twelve points may appear straightforward, but they represent the bedrock of a robust business credit foundation. They also encapsulate a core message that was passed throughout this book: **Success in credit management comes from intentional planning, meticulous attention to detail, and unwavering commitment to doing things the right way from the start.**

REFLECTING ON THE BIGGER PICTURE

Throughout the book, each chapter has provided actionable insights:

- **The Basics of Business Credit:** You discovered that strong business credit is not simply about borrowing money. It is about establishing credibility, protecting personal assets, and creating a foundation for future growth.

- **Establishing Your Business Credit Profile:** Step by step, you learned how to formalize your business, set up professional operations, and build the critical elements that form a robust credit profile.

- **Understanding Business Credit Scores:** You gained a clear picture of how credit scores work, the key components that influence them, and the importance of regular monitoring to ensure accuracy.

- **Trade Lines and Vendor Accounts:** Like tending to a well-cared-for garden, building trade lines and vendor accounts is essential. You explored how these relationships are nurtured through disciplined payments and strategic vendor selections.

Shameka Landers

- **Leveraging Business Credit for Growth and Scaling Your Business:** These chapters illustrated how credit can serve as the lifeblood for expansion—whether it's funding inventory, hiring talent, or entering new markets. You learned that scaling a business requires not just access to credit but also careful planning and execution.

- **Managing Debt and Avoiding Common Pitfalls:** The strategies for responsible debt management highlighted the importance of clear financial boundaries, disciplined repayment, and proactive monitoring. Avoiding mistakes such as over-leveraging or mixing personal and business finances is crucial for long-term stability.

- **Smart Financial Management:** With budgeting, cash flow optimization, and cost management as central themes, you discovered that effective financial management is the backbone of a thriving business.

- **The Future of Business Credit:** You explored emerging trends—from fintech innovations and blockchain to open banking—reminding you that the landscape is evolving and that staying informed is key.

- **Leveraging Credit for Competitive Advantage:** Here, the focus was on using a strong credit profile to secure better terms, negotiate with confidence, and even expand internationally, thereby transforming credit into a strategic asset.

- **Risk Management in Credit Use:** The importance of balancing opportunity with caution was underscored. You learned to assess risks, build financial buffers, and implement proactive measures to safeguard your credit profile.

- **Using Business Credit to Improve Operations:** Investing in technology, streamlining processes, and enhancing supply chain efficiency are ways to ensure that every dollar borrowed works smarter for your business.

- **How Successful Entrepreneurs Use Business Credit:** Real-life case studies demonstrated that the most successful business leaders view credit not as a burden but as a catalyst for strategic growth and innovation.

- **Smart Leadership and Team Management:** Financial literacy, accountability, and transparency within leadership teams were highlighted as cornerstones of sustained financial success.

- **Transitioning from Credit Reliance to Financial Independence:** Recognizing the signs that your business is ready to rely less on credit and more on retained earnings is a significant milestone in achieving long-term financial independence.

- **The Legacy of Smart Credit Use:** Finally, building a lasting financial legacy is about more than immediate gains—it's about setting a foundation for future generations, ensuring that the principles of responsible credit management continue to propel your business forward.

KEY REFLECTIONS AND TAKEAWAYS

As you close this guide, take a moment to reflect on the actionable strategies and case studies that have been shared. Consider these essential takeaways:

- **Financial Discipline:** Every prompt payment, strategic investment, and cautious borrowing decision reinforces your business's financial health.

- **Strategic Borrowing:** Use credit as a lever to seize opportunities—whether that means expanding into new markets, upgrading technology, or negotiating better supplier terms.

- **Risk and Resilience:** Proactive risk management, including maintaining emergency funds and diversifying credit sources, ensures that your business can weather economic uncertainties.

- **Continuous Improvement:** The world of business credit is ever-evolving. Regularly review your strategies, stay updated on industry trends, and foster a culture of financial literacy within your team.

- **Legacy Building:** Responsible credit management today paves the way for sustained growth and creates a legacy that benefits future generations of business leaders.

A CALL TO ACTION

The insights provided throughout this book are more than mere information—they are a call to action. Every chapter has equipped you with the tools to evaluate your current financial practices, identify areas for improvement, and implement strategies that can transform your business credit into a formidable asset.

Now is the time to put these strategies into practice. Review your financial policies, engage your team in discussions about credit management, and start setting measurable goals for your business's financial future. Remember, each decision you make today has the power to reshape your tomorrow.

Embrace the mindset that credit, when managed with discipline and foresight, is not a burden but a bridge—a bridge to greater opportunities, stronger partnerships, and a legacy of financial empowerment.

Thank you for joining this journey toward smarter business practices and enhanced financial literacy. Your story of success is waiting to be written, and with the principles of smart credit use at your side, there is no limit to what you can achieve.

Let your credit be the catalyst that propels your business into a future defined by resilience, growth, and lasting success.

Shameka Landers

Made in the USA
Columbia, SC
15 April 2025